MW01120133

Cardinal Wolsey

Twelve English Statesmen

CARDINAL WOLSEY

BY

MANDELL CREIGHTON

BISHOP OF LONDON
M.A. OXFORD AND CAMBRIDGE, D C.L. OF DURHAM
LL D. OF GLASGOW AND HARVARD

MACMILLAN AND CO., LIMITED
ST. MARTIN'S STREET. LONDON

1921

First Edition April 1888
Reprinted 1888, 1891, 1895, 1898, 1902, 1904, 1906 (*twice*), 1912
1921

CONTENTS

CHAPTER I

THE STATE OF EUROPE, 1494-1512 1

CHAPTER II

THE FRENCH ALLIANCE, 1512-1515 18

CHAPTER III

THE UNIVERSAL PEACE, 1515-1518 35

CHAPTER IV

THE FIELD OF THE CLOTH OF GOLD, 1518-1520 . . . 51

CHAPTER V

THE CONFERENCE OF CALAIS, 1520-1521 66

CHAPTER VI

THE IMPERIAL ALLIANCE, 1521-1523 . . . 84

CHAPTER VII

Renewal of Peace, 1523-1527 . . . . .

CHAPTER VIII

Wolsey's Domestic Policy . . . . . .

CHAPTER IX

The King's Divorce, 1527-1529 . . . . .

CHAPTER X

The Fall of Wolsey, 1529-1530 . . . . .

CHAPTER XI

The Work of Wolsey . . . .

CHAPTER I

ALL men are to be judged by what they do, and the way in which they do it. In the case of great statesmen there is a third consideration which challenges our judgment —what they choose to do. This consideration only presents itself in the case of great statesmen, and even then is not always recognised. For the average statesman does from day to day the business which has to be done, takes affairs as he finds them, and makes the best of them. Many who deliberately selected the questions with which they dealt have yet shrunk from the responsibility of their choice, and have preferred to represent their actions as inevitable. Few can claim the credit of choosing the sphere of their activity, of framing a connected policy with clear and definite ends, and of applying their ideas to every department of national organisation. In short, statesmen are generally opportunists, or choose to represent themselves as such; and this has been especially the case with English statesmen—amongst whom Wolsey stands out as a notable exception. For Wolsey claims recognition on grounds which apply to

B

himself alone.   His name is not associated with any great
achievement, he worked out no great measure of reform,
nor did he contribute any great political idea which was
fruitful in after days.   He was, above all things, a practical man, though he pursued a line of policy which few
understood, and which he did not stop to make intelligible.   No very definite results came of it immediately,
and the results which came of it afterwards were not
such as Wolsey had designed.   Yet, if we consider his
actual achievements, we are bound to admit that he was
probably the greatest political genius whom England has
ever produced ; for at a great crisis of European history
he impressed England with a sense of her own importance,
and secured for her a leading position in European
affairs, which since his days has seemed her natural
right.

Thus Wolsey is to be estimated by what he chose to
do rather than by what he did.   He was greater than
his achievements.   Yet Wolsey's greatness did not rise
beyond the conditions of his own age, and he left no
legacy of great thought or high endeavour.   The age in
which he lived was not one of lofty aspirations or noble
aims ; but it was one of large designs and restless energy.
No designs were cast in so large a mould as were those
of Wolsey ; no statesman showed such skill as he did in
weaving patiently the web of diplomatic intrigue.   His
resources were small, and he husbanded them with care.
He had a master who only dimly understood his objects,
and whose personal whims and caprices had always to
be conciliated.   He was ill supplied with agents.   His
schemes often failed in detail ; but he was always ready
to gather together the broken threads and resume his

work without repining. In a time of universal restlessness and excitement Wolsey was the most plodding, the most laborious, and the most versatile of those who laboured at statecraft.

The field of action which Wolsey deliberately chose was that of foreign policy, and his weapons were diplomacy. The Englishmen of his time were like the Englishmen of to-day, and had little sympathy with his objects. Those who reaped the benefits of his policy gave him no thanks for it, nor did they recognise what they owed to him. Those who exulted in the course taken by the English Reformation regarded Wolsey as its bitterest foe, and never stopped to think that Wolsey trained the hands and brains which directed it; that Wolsey inspired England with the proud feeling of independence which nerved her to brave the public opinion of Europe; that Wolsey impressed Europe with such a sense of England's greatness that she was allowed to go her own way, menaced but unassailed. The spirit which animated the England of the sixteenth century was due in no small degree to the splendour of Wolsey's successes, and to the way in which he stamped upon men's imagination a belief in England's greatness. If it is the characteristic of a patriot to believe that nothing is beyond the power of his country to achieve, then Wolsey was the most devoted patriot whom England ever produced.

When Wolsey came to power England was an upstart trying to claim for herself a decent position in the august society of European states. It was Wolsey's cleverness that set her in a place far above that which she had any right to expect. For this purpose Wolsey

schemed and intrigued ; when one plan failed he was
always ready with another.   It mattered little what was
the immediate object which he had in hand ; it mattered
much that in pursuing it he should so act as to increase
the credit of England, and create a belief in England's
power.   Diplomacy can reckon few abler practitioners
than was Wolsey.

There is little that is directly ennobling in the con-
templation of such a career.   It may be doubted if the
career of any practical statesman can be a really ennobling study if we have all its activity recorded in
detail.   At the best it tells us of much which seems
disingenuous if not dishonest—much in which nobility
of aim or the complexity of affairs has to be urged in
extenuation of shifty words and ambiguous actions.

The age in which Wolsey lived was immoral in the
sense in which all periods are immoral, when the old
landmarks are disappearing and there is no certainty
about the future.   Morality in individuals and in states
alike requires an orderly life, a perception of limits, a
pursuit of definite ends.   When order is shattered,
when limits are removed, when all things seem possible,
then political morality disappears.   In such a condition
was Europe at the beginning of the sixteenth century.
The old ideas, on which the mediæval conception of
Christendom depended, were passing away.   No one any
longer regarded Christendom as one great commonwealth, presided over by Pope and Emperor, who were the
guardians of international law and arbiters of international relations.   The Empire had long ceased to exercise
any control, because it was destitute of strength.   The
Papacy, after vainly endeavouring to unite Europe round

the old cry of a crusade against the Turk, had discovered
that there was no European power on which it could
rely for support. The old ideas were gone, the old
tribunals were powerless, the old bonds of European
union were dissolved.

The first result of this decay in the mediæval state-
system of Europe was the emergence of vague plans of
a universal monarchy. The Empire and the Papacy had
harmonised with the feudal conception of a regulative
supremacy over vassals who were free to act within the
limits of their obligations to their superior lord. When
the old superiors were no longer recognised, the idea of
a supremacy still remained; but there was no other
basis possible for that supremacy than a basis of universal sovereignty. It was long before any state was
sufficiently powerful to venture on such a claim; but the
end of the fifteenth century saw France and Spain
united into powerful kingdoms. In France, the policy
of Louis XI. succeeded in reducing the great feudatories, and established the power of the monarchy as the
bond of union between provinces which were conscious
of like interests. In Spain, the marriage of Ferdinand
and Isabella united a warlike people who swept away
the remains of the Moorish kingdom. Germany, though
nominally it recognised one ruler, had sacrificed its
national kingship to the futile claims of the Empire
The emperor had great pretensions, but was himself
powerless, and the German princes steadily refused to
lend him help to give reality to his high-sounding
claims. Unconsciously to themselves, the rulers of
France and Spain were preparing to attempt the extension of their power over the rest of Europe.

France under Charles VIII. was the first to give
expression to this new idea of European politics. The
Italian expedition of Charles VIII. marked the end
of the Middle Ages, because it put forth a scheme
of national aggrandisement which was foreign to
mediæval conceptions. The scheme sounded fantastic,
and was still cast in the mould of mediæval aspirations.
The kingdom of Naples had long been in dispute
between the houses of Arragon and Anjou. As heir
to the Angevin line, Charles VIII. proposed to satisfy
national pride by the conquest of Naples. Then he
appealed to the old sentiment of Christendom by pro-
claiming his design of advancing against Constantinople,
expelling the Turk from Europe, and realising the ideal
of mediæval Christianity by planting once more the
standard of the Cross upon the Holy Sepulchre at
Jerusalem.

The first part of his plan succeeded with a rapidity
and ease that bewildered the rest of Europe. The
French conquest of Naples awakened men to the danger
which threatened them. France, as ruler of Naples,
could overrun the rest of Italy, and as master of the
Pope could use the authority of the head of Christendom to give legitimacy to further schemes of aggression.
A sense of common danger drew the other powers of
Europe together; and a League of Spain, the Empire,
the Pope, Milan, and Venice forced Charles VIII. to
retire from Naples (1495), where the French conquests
were rapidly lost. A threat of his return next year led
to an emphatic renewal of the League and an assertion
of the basis on which it rested—"the mutual preservation of states, so that the more powerful might not

oppress the less powerful, and that each should keep what rightly belongs to him."

This League marks a new departure in European affairs. There was no mention of the old ideas on which Europe was supposed to rest. There was no recognition of papal or imperial supremacy; no principle of European organisation was laid down. The existing state of things was to be maintained, and the contracting powers were to decide amongst themselves what rights and claims they thought fit to recognise. Such a plan might be useful to check French preponderance at the moment, but it was fatal to the free development of Europe. The states that were then powerful might grow in power; those that were not yet strong were sure to be prevented from growing stronger. Dynastic interests were set up as against national interests. . European affairs were to be settled by combinations of powerful states.

The results of this system were rapidly seen. France, of course, was checked for the time; but France, in its turn, could enter the League and become a factor in European combinations. The problem now for statesmen was how to use this concert of Europe for their own interests. Dynastic considerations were the most obvious means of gaining powerful alliances. Royal marriages became matters of the greatest importance, because a lucky union of royal houses might secure a lasting preponderance. The Emperor Maximilian married his son Philip to a daughter of Ferdinand and Isabella. Death removed the nearer heirs to the Spanish rulers, and the son of Philip was heir to Austria, the Netherlands, and the Spanish kingdoms. The notion of a maintenance of European equilibrium faded away before such a prospect.

This prospect, however, was only in the future. For the present there was an opportunity for endless scheming. The European League for the preservation of the existing state of things resisted any expansion on the part of smaller states, but encouraged compacts for aggression amongst the more powerful. France, Spain, and Germany had each of them a national existence, while Italy consisted of a number of small states. If Italy was to survive it was necessary that she should follow the example of her powerful neighbours, and consolidate herself as they had done. The only state which was at that time likely to unite Italy was Venice; and Venice, in consequence, became the object of universal jealousy. The concert of Europe was applied to the Venetian question, and discovered a solution of the simplest sort. Instead of allowing Venice to unite Italy, it was judged better to divide Venice. A secret agreement was made between Spain, France, the Emperor, and the Pope that they would attack Venice simultaneously, deprive her of her possessions, and divide them amongst themselves. There was no lack of claims and titles to the possessions which were thus to be acquired. The powers of Europe, being judges in their own cause, could easily state their respective pleas and pronounce each other justified. The League of Cambrai, which was published at the end of 1508, was the first great production of the new system of administering public law in Europe.

Anything more iniquitous could scarcely be conceived. Venice deserved well at the hands of Europe. She had developed a great system of commerce with the East;

she was the chief bulwark against the advance of the
Turkish power; she was the one refuge of Italian
independence. Those very reasons marked her out for
pillage by the powers who, claiming to act in the
interests of Europe, interpreted these interests according to their own selfishness. Each power hoped to
appropriate some of the profits of Venetian commerce;
each power wished for a slice of the domains of Italy.
What the Turk did was a matter of little consequence;
he was not the object of immediate dread.

This League of Cambrai witnessed the assimilation
by the new system of the relics of the old. Imperial
and papal claims were set in the foreground. Venice
was excommunicated by the Pope, because she had the
audacity to refuse to give up to him at once his share of
the booty. The iniquities of the European concert were
flimsily concealed by the rags of the old system of the
public law of Europe, which only meant that the Pope
and the Emperor were foremost in joining in the general
scramble. France was first in the field against Venice,
and consequently France was the chief gainer. Pope
Julius II., having won from Venice all that he could
claim, looked with alarm on the increase of the French
power in Italy. As soon as he had satisfied himself, and
had reduced Venice to abject submission, his one desire
was to rid himself of his troublesome allies. The papal
authority in itself could no longer influence European
politics; but it could give a sanction to new combinations which interested motives might bring about.
With cynical frankness the Papacy, powerless in its own
resources, used its privileged position to further its
temporal objects. We cannot wonder that Louis XII.

of France tried to create a schism, and promoted the
holding of a general council. We are scarcely surprised
that the fantastic brain of the Emperor Maximilian
formed a scheme of becoming the Pope's coadjutor, and
finally annexing the papal to the imperial dignity. On
every side the old landmarks of Europe were disappearing, and the future was seen to belong to the strong
hand and the adventurous wit.

During the reign of Henry VII. England had stood
aloof from these complicated intrigues. Indeed England
could not hope to make her voice heard in the affairs of
Europe. The weak government of Henry VI., and the
struggles between the Yorkist and Lancastrian factions,
had reduced her to political exhaustion. While France
and Spain had grown into strong kingdoms, England
had dwindled into a third-rate power. Henry VII.
had enough to do in securing his own throne against
pretenders, and in reducing the remnants of the feudal
nobility to obedience. He so far worked in accordance
with the prevailing spirit that he steadily increased the
royal power. He fell in with the temper of the time,
and formed matrimonial alliances which might bear
political fruits. He gave his daughter in marriage to
the King of Scotland, in the hopes of thereby bringing
the Scottish Crown into closer relation with England.
He sought for a connexion with Spain by marrying his
eldest son Arthur to Katharine, a daughter of Ferdinand
and Isabella, and on Arthur's untimely death Katharine
became the wife of his next son Henry. Further,
Henry VII. gave his general approval to the League of
1496 ; he joined it, but would promise no armed aid nor
money. In short, he did enough to claim for England

a place in the new system of the European commonwealth, though he himself declined to take any active
part in the activity that was consequently developed.
He was old before his years, and was unequal to any
additional labour. He had saved his reputation by his
cautious and skilful policy at home. The statesmen of
Europe respected him for what he had done already,
but they did not expect him to do anything more. He
had secured his dynasty, reduced his lands to order,
favoured its commerce, and secured for it peace. He
had lived frugally and had saved money, which was not
the fortune of the more adventurous princes. England
was looked upon with an eye of condescending favour
by the great powers of Europe. Her population was
small, about three millions and a half; her military
forces had not been trained in the new methods of
European warfare; her navy was not kept up on a war
footing. She could not rank higher than a third-rate
power.

So England stood when Henry VII. died, and was
succeeded by his son Henry VIII., a youth of nineteen.
We may indulge ourselves, if we choose, in speculations
on the probable effects if Henry VIII. had been content
to pursue his father's policy. The picture of England,
peaceful and contented while the rest of Europe is engaged in wasteful and wicked war, is attractive as an ideal
in English politics. England in the sixteenth century
might have stood aloof from European affairs, and might
have prospered in her own fashion. But one thing is
certain, that she would never have become the England
of to-day; the New World, and the possessions of the
British Empire, would have been divided between France

and Spain; the course of civilisation would have been
widely different. For good or for evil the fortunes of
England were given a decided direction by Henry VIII.'s
advance into the sphere of European politics. England
took up a position from which she could not afterwards
retire.

It is scarcely worth while to inquire if Henry VIII.
could by prudence and caution have continued to keep
clear of the complications of European politics, and
make England strong by husbanding its resources and
developing its commerce. Such a course of action was
not deemed possible by any one. All classes alike
believed that national prosperity followed upon the
assertion of national power. The commercial interests
of England would have had little chance of being respected unless they were connected with political interests
as well. If Henry VIII. had lived frugally like his
father, and avoided adventurous schemes for which he
needed the money of his people, the English monarchy
would have become a despotism, and the royal will
would have been supreme in all internal affairs. England was not exposed to this danger. Henry VIII.,
when he ascended the throne at the age of nineteen,
was fully imbued by the spirit of his time. The story
goes that when Leo X. was elected Pope he turned to
his brother and said with a smile, "Let us enjoy the
Papacy, since God has given it to us." Henry VIII.
was resolved to enjoy his kingship to the full; he
wished to show Europe that he was every inch a king,
and equal to the best.

Henry VIII. in his early days had been educated
with a view to high ecclesiastical preferment, and was a

youth of many accomplishments of mind and body. His tall stalwart frame, his fair round face and profusion of light hair, his skill in athletic exercises, made the Venetian envoy pronounce him to be the handsomest and most capable king in Christendom. He inherited the geniality, the physical strength, the resoluteness of the Yorkist house, and combined them with the self-restraint and caution of the Lancastrians. No king began his reign with greater popularity, and the belief in the soundness of his head and heart filled all men with hopes of a long period of just and prosperous government. But many hoped for more than this. The reign of Henry VII. had been successful, but inglorious The strong character and the generous impulses of the new ruler were not likely to be satisfied with the cautious intrigues and petty calculations of his father. England looked forward to a glorious and distinguished future. It believed in its king, and clave to its belief in spite of many disappointments. Not all the harsh doings of Henry VIII. exhausted the popularity with which he began his reign, and in the midst of his despotism he never lost his hold upon the people.

So Henry VIII. carried out the plan which his father had formed for him. He married Katharine, his brother's widow, and so confirmed the alliance with Ferdinand of Spain. He renewed the marriage treaty between his sister Mary and Charles, Prince of Castile, heir of the Netherlands, and eldest grandson of Ferdinand and Maximilian alike. Charles was only a boy of nine, and had great prospects of a large heritage. England was likely, if this arrangement were carried out, to be a useful but humble ally to the projects of the houses

of Hapsburg and Spain, useful because of its position,
which commanded the Channel, and could secure communications between the Netherlands and Spain, humble
because it had little military reputation or capacity for
diplomacy.

The alliance, however, between Ferdinand and
Maximilian was by no means close. Ferdinand by his
marriage with Isabella had united the kingdoms of
Castile and Arragon; but after Isabella's death he had
no claim to the Crown of Castile, which passed to his
daughter Juana. Already Juana's husband, the Archduke Philip, had claimed the regency of Castile, and
Ferdinand was only saved by Philip's death from the
peril of seeing much of his work undone. The claim to
Castile had now passed to the young Charles, and
Ferdinand was afraid lest Maximilian should at any
time revive it in behalf of his grandson. He was unwilling to help in any way to increase Maximilian's
power, and rejoiced that in the results of the League
of Cambrai little profit fell to Maximilian's share. The
Pope gained all that he wished ; Ferdinand acquired
without a blow the Venetian possessions in the Neapoli-
tan kingdom; the French arms were triumphant in
North Italy; but Venice continued to offer a stubborn
resistance to Maximilian. In vain Maximilian implored
Ferdinand's help. He was unmoved till the successes
of the French awakened in his .mind serious alarm.
The authors of the League of Cambrai began to be
afraid of the catastrophe which they had caused. They
did not wish to see the French supreme in Italy, but
their combination had gone far to ensure the French
supremacy.

Pope Julius II. felt himself most directly threatened
by the growth of the French power. He resolved to
break up the League of Cambrai, and so undo his own
work. He tried to gain support from the Swiss and
from England   He released Venice from her excom-
munication, and showed himself steadfastly opposed to
France. He did his utmost to induce Ferdinand and
Maximilian to renounce the League. Ferdinand was
cautious, and only gave his secret countenance to the
Pope's designs. Maximilian, anxious to make good his
claims against Venice, wavered between an alliance with
France and a rupture. Louis XII. of France was embarrassed by the hostility of the Pope, whom he tried
to terrify into submission   His troops advanced against
Bologna, where Julius II. was residing. The Pope fled,
but the French forces did not pursue him. Louis was
not prepared to treat the Pope as merely a temporal
sovereign, and Rome was spared a siege. But Louis
was so ill-judging as to attack the Pope on his spiritual
side. He raised the old cry of a General Council for the
reform of the Church, and drew to his side a few dis-
affected cardinals, who summoned a Council to assemble
at Pisa.

This half-hearted procedure was fatal to all hopes of
French supremacy. Had Louis XII. promptly dealt
with Julius II. by force of arms he would have rendered
the Pope powerless to interfere with his political plans,
and no one would have interposed to help the Pope
in his capacity of an Italian prince. But when the
French king showed that he was afraid of the papal
dignity in temporal matters, while he was ready to
attack it in spiritual matters, he entered upon a course

of action which was dangerous to Europe. Ferdinand was waiting for a good pretext to free himself from further share in the policy of the League of Cambrai, and Louis provided him with the pretext which he sought. Shocked at the danger of a new schism, Ferdinand, in October 1511, entered into a League with the Pope and Venice, a League which took the high-sounding title of the Holy League, since it was formed for the protection of the Papacy.

Of this Holy League Henry VIII. became a member in December, and so stepped boldly into the politics of Europe. He was at first a submissive son of King Ferdinand, whose daughter, Queen Katharine, acted as Spanish ambassador at the English Court. Henry wished to make common cause with his father-in-law, and trusted implicitly to him for assurances of goodwill. He made a separate accord with Ferdinand that a combined army should invade Guienne. If the French were defeated Ferdinand would be able to conquer Navarre, and England would seize Guienne. The gain to England would be great, as Guienne would be a secure refuge for English commerce, and its possession would make the English king an important personage in Europe, for he would stand between Spain and France.

The scheme was not fantastic or impossible, provided that Ferdinand was in earnest. Henry believed in his good faith, but he still had the confidence of youth. Ferdinand trusted no one, and if others were like himself he was wise in his distrust. Every year he grew more suspicious and fonder of crooked ways. He took no man's counsel; he made fair professions on every side ; his only object was to secure himself at the least cost. His confiding son-in-law was soon to discover that Ferdinand only meant to use English gold as a means for furthering his own designs against France ; he did not intend that England should have any share in the advantage.

Unconscious of the selfishness of his ally, Henry VIII prepared for war in the winter of 1512. In these preparations the capacity of Thomas Wolsey first made itself felt, and the course of the war that followed placed Wolsey foremost in the confidence of the English king.

CHAPTER II

THOMAS WOLSEY was born at Ipswich, probably in March 1471. He was the son of Robert Wolsey and Joan his wife. Contemporary slander, wishing to make his fortunes more remarkable or his presumption more intolerable, represented his father as a man of mean estate, a butcher by trade. However, Robert Wolsey's will shows that he was a man of good position, probably a grazier and wool merchant, with relatives who were also well-to-do. Thomas seems to have been the eldest of his family, and his father's desire was that he should enter the priesthood. He showed quickness in study; so much so that he went to Oxford at the early age of eleven, and became Bachelor of Arts when he was fifteen. His studies do not·seem to have led him in the direction of the new learning; he was well versed in the theology of the schools, and is said to have been a devoted adherent to the system of St. Thomas Aquinas. But it was not by the life of a student or the principles of a philosopher that Wolsey rose to eminence. If he learned anything in his University career he learned a knowledge of men and of their motives.

In due course he became a Fellow of Magdalen, and master of the grammar school attached to the College. Soon afterwards, in 1498, he was bursar; and tradition has connected with him the building of the graceful tower which is one of the chief architectural ornaments of Oxford. Unfortunately the tower was finished in the year in which Wolsey became bursar, and all that he can have done was the prosaic duty of paying the bills for its erection. He continued his work of schoolmaster till in 1500 the Marquis of Dorset, whose sons Wolsey had taught, gave him the living of Lymington in Somerset.

So Wolsey abandoned academic life for the quietness of a country living, which, however, did not prove to be entirely free from troubles. For some reason which is not clear, a neighbouring squire, Sir Amyas Paulet, used his power as justice of peace to set Wolsey in the stocks, an affront which Wolsey did not forgive, but in the days of his power punished by confining Sir Amyas to his London house, where he lived for some years in disgrace. If this story be true, it is certainly not to Wolsey's discredit, who can have been moved by nothing but a sense of injustice in thus reviving the remembrance of his own past history. Moreover, Wolsey's character certainly did not suffer at the time, as in 1501 he was made chaplain to Dean, Archbishop of Canterbury. After Dean's death in 1503, his capacity for business was so far established that he was employed by Sir Richard Nanfan, Deputy-Lieutenant of Calais, to help him in the duties of a post which advancing years made

somewhat onerous. When Nanfan, a few years after
wards, retired from public life, he recommended Wolsey
to the king, and Wolsey entered the royal service as
chaplain probably in 1506.

At Court Wolsey allied himself with Richard Fox,
Bishop of Winchester, Lord Privy Seal, and at first
seems to have acted as one of his secretaries.

Fox was a well-trained and careful official, who had
been in Henry VII.'s employment all through his reign.
Cold and cautious by nature, Henry VII. had to pick
his way through many difficulties, and took no man unreservedly into his confidence. He was his own minister,
and chose to be served by men of distinguished position
who were content to do his bidding faithfully, and were
free from personal ambition. For this purpose ecclesiastics were best adapted, and Henry VII. did much to
secularise the Church by throwing the weight of public
business into the hands of men like Morton and Fox,
whom he rewarded by the highest ecclesiastical offices.
In such a school Wolsey was trained as a statesman.
He regarded it as natural that the King should choose
his ministers for their readiness to serve his purposes,
and should reward them by ecclesiastical preferments.
The State might gain by such a plan, but the Church
undoubtedly lost; and in following the career of Wolsey
there is little to remind us of the ecclesiastic, however
much we may admire the statesman.

It was well for England that Wolsey was trained in
the traditions of the policy of Henry VII., which he
never forgot. Henry VII. aimed, in the first place, at
securing his throne and restoring quiet and order in his
kingdom by developing trade and commerce. For this

purpose he strove to turn his foreign neighbours into allies without adventuring into any military enterprises. He did not aspire to make England great, but he tried to make her secure and prosperous. Wolsey gained so much insight into the means which he employed for that end that he never forgot their utility; and though he tried to pass beyond the aim of Henry VII., he preferred to extend rather than abandon the means which Henry VII. had carefully devised. Nor was Wolsey merely a spectator of Henry VII.'s diplomacy; he was soon employed as one of its agents. In the spring of 1508 he was sent to Scotland to keep King James IV. true to his alliance with England, and explain misunderstandings that had arisen. In the autumn of the same year he was sent to Mechlin to win over the powerful minister of Maximilian, the Bishop of Gurk, to a project of marriage between Henry VII. and Maximilian's daughter Margaret, by which Henry hoped that he would get control of the Low Countries. Here Wolsey learned his first practical lesson of diplomatic methods, and uttered the complaint, which in later years he gave so much reason to others to pour forth, "There is here so much inconstancy, mutability, and little regard of promises and causes, that in their appointments there is little trust or surety; for things surely determined to be done one day are changed and altered the next."

Nothing came of Wolsey's embassy, nor can we be sure that Henry VII. was much in earnest in his marriage schemes. However, he died in April next year, and was succeeded by a son whose matrimonial hesitations were destined to give Wolsey more trouble than those of his father. Before his death he laid the

foundation of Wolsey's clerical fortunes by bestowing
on him the rich deanery of Lincoln.

The accession of Henry VIII. made little change in
the composition of the King's Council.   The Lady
Margaret survived her son long enough to make her influence felt in the choice of her grandson's advisers.
Archbishop Warham, Bishop Fox, and Thomas Howard,
Earl of Surrey, were the men into whose hands public
business naturally fell.   But Warham was somewhat
stiff and crabbed, so that he did not commend himself
to the young king.   Fox represented the opinions of
the old officials, while the Earl of Surrey was the natural
leader of the old nobility, who could not help resenting
the subordinate position into which they had been reduced by Henry VII., and hoped that a new reign would
give them fresh opportunities.   So Fox urged caution
and carefulness, while Surrey favoured extravagance and
military ambition.- Fox felt that he was growing old,
and the pressure of a continued conflict of opinion was
irksome to him.   Much as the ecclesiastics of that time
were secular in their lives, they were rarely entirely for-
getful of their priestly office, and were genuinely anxious
to rid themselves of the burden of affairs and spend their
last years in quiet.   So Fox chose Wolsey as the man
to take his place, perhaps because he saw in him the
qualities necessary to influence the young king.   Besides
him he favoured Ruthal, another experienced official,
who was rewarded by the rich bishopric of Durham, but
who was soon eclipsed by the superior genius of Wolsey,
which he frankly admitted, and willingly accepted the
post of Wolsey's assistant and subordinate.

So Wolsey was made the king's almoner, and had

sundry preferments bestowed on him as marks of the
royal favour. He ingratiated himself with the king,
and worked with Fox and Ruthal to counteract the influence of the Earl of Surrey. Probably in 1511 he
was called to the King's Council, but neither he nor
Fox had it in their power to shape the king's policy as
they wished, or to direct his doings. His warlike ardour
was against their will; but from the beginning of his
reign Henry VIII. went his own way, and others had to
follow. All they could do was to show him that they
were the most capable of his servants, and when Henry
VIII. had determined on war they were the men to
whom he turned to carry out the necessary details. On
Wolsey as the youngest the chief labour was thrown.
England was unprepared for war, and every branch of
the military service had to be almost created. Wolsey
had at all events a sufficient opportunity for displaying
his practical capacity as an organiser.

So Wolsey worked at providing for the troops who
were sent to Guienne in 1512; but the expedition
itself was a complete failure. Ferdinand played his own
game of procrastination, and sent no succours. The
Marquis of Dorset was an incapable leader. The English
troops were not inured to hardships, and soon grew
discontented; at last they rose in open mutiny, and
clamoured to be led back to England. Dorset was
driven to retire without striking a blow. The first
attempt of England to assert her prowess ended in
disaster. The statesmen of the Continent made merry
over the blundering efforts of an upstart power.
"The English," they said, "are so unaccustomed to war
that they have no experience to guide them." Henry

longed to wipe out this disgrace, and prepared to
invade the north of France in the next year. Wolsey
was not yet of sufficient importance to direct the
king's policy, and had no experience of war. But
he threw himself heart and soul into the task of
military organisation, and the administrative capacity
which he displayed secured his hold on the king's
favour. He provided for victualling the fleet, raised the
necessary number of ships, selected their captains, and
even apportioned the gunners. Nothing was too trivial
for his attention, even down to beer-barrels and biscuits.
It is not surprising that his colleague, Bishop Fox, wrote
to him, "I pray God send us with speed, and soon deliver
you of your outrageous charge and labour."

The fleet put to sea in March 1513, under the command of the Lord Admiral Sir Edward Howard. The
French fleet was far superior in numbers, and prepared
to prevent the English from landing on the French
coast. Sir Edward Howard was burning with desire
for a decisive engagement, and on 25th April attacked
the French galleys as they lay in shallow water.
He boarded them with his boats, and himself leapt
on to the ship of the French admiral, but before his
men could follow him their cable was cut away, and he
was left almost alone. Seeing that there was no hope
of support, he took his whistle from his neck and cast
it into the sea; then with his gilt target on his arm he
fought till the enemy's pikes thrust him overboard and
he was drowned. The English attack was driven back;
but its gallantry and the bravery of Sir Edward Howard
produced a great impression. It was clear that after
all the Englishmen had not forgotten how to fight.

The efforts of the English fleet were successful in securing the peaceful landing of the army at Calais, where Henry arrived at the end of June. With him went Wolsey, commanding two hundred men, and now a necessary personage in the king's train. Such confidence was placed in him by Queen Katharine that she requested him to write to her frequently and inform her of the king's health, while in return she poured her household troubles into his sympathetic ear. No doubt Wolsey's hands were full of business of many kinds during this brief and glorious campaign, glorious in the sense that success attended its operations, but fruitless because the things done were scarcely worth the doing. The English army took Terouenne, more owing to the feebleness of the French than to their own valour. Louis XII. was prematurely old and ailing; things had gone against him in Italy, and there was little spirit in the French army. The defeat of the French outside Terouenne was so rapid that the battle was derisively called the Battle of Spurs. Henry's desire for martial glory was satisfied by the surrender of Terouenne, and his vanity was gratified by the presence of Maximilian, who in return for a large subsidy brought a few German soldiers, and professed to serve under the English king. From Terouenne he advanced to Tournai, which surrendered at the end of September. Maximilian was delighted at these conquests, of which he reaped all the benefit; with Tournai in the hands of England, Flanders had a strong protection against France. So Maximilian would gladly have led Henry to continue the campaign in the interests of the Flemish frontier. But Henry had no taste for spending a winter in the field; he pleaded that his presence was needed in England, and departed, promising to return next year.

In truth the arms of England had won a greater victory on English ground than anything they had achieved abroad. The war against France awakened the old hostility of Scotland, and no sooner was Henry VIII. encamped before Terouenne than he received a Scottish herald bringing a message of defiance. "I do not believe that my brother of Scotland will break his oath," said Henry, "but if he does, he will live to repent it." Repentance came rapidly on the Field of Flodden, where the Scottish army was almost cut to pieces. This brilliant victory was greatly due to the energy of Queen Katharine, who wrote to Wolsey, "My heart is very good to it, and I am horribly busy with making standards, banners, and badges." She addressed the English leaders before they started for the war, bade them remember that the English courage excelled that of other nations, and that the Lord smiled on those who stood in defence of their own. With a proud heart she sent her husband the blood-stained plaid of the Scottish king, taken from his corpse. "In this," she wrote, "your Grace shall see how I keep my promise, sending you for your banner a king's coat."

The victory of Flodden Field was of great importance, for it delivered England from the fear of a troublesome neighbour, and showed Europe that England could not be muzzled by the need of care for her own borders. The Scottish power was broken for many years to come, and England was free to act as she would. Europe began to respect the power of England, though there was little reason to rate highly the wisdom of her king. Henry had won little by his campaign ; he had gratified his vanity, but he had not advanced towards any definite end.

Henry VIII. was young and simple. He expected to captivate the world by brilliant deeds, and fascinate it by unselfish exploits. He soon found that his pretended allies were only seeking their own advantage. The name of the "Holy League" was the merest pretext. The new Pope, Leo X., a supple time-serving intriguer, trained in the deceitful policy of the Medici House, was willing to patch up the quarrel between France and the Papacy. Ferdinand of Spain wished only to keep things as they were. As he grew older he grew more suspicious, and clung to the power which he possessed. His one dread was lest Charles, the grandson of himself and Maximilian, should demand his maternal heritage of Castile. Ferdinand was resolved to keep the two Spanish kingdoms united under his own rule until his death, and considered European affairs in the first instance as they were likely to affect that issue. He was of opinion that France was no longer formidable to Spanish interests in Italy, while English successes on the Flemish frontier might make Charles more powerful than he wished him to be. Accordingly he set to work to undermine Henry's position by making an alliance with France. He was still Henry's ally, and had promised him to help him to continue the war in the spring of 1514. None the less he entered into secret negotiations with France, and cautiously endeavoured to persuade Maximilian to join him. Maximilian was still at war with Venice, and was aggrieved that he was the only member of the plundering gang who had not gained by the League of Cambrai. Ferdinand allured him from his interest in Flanders by the prospect of a renewal of the League against Venice in his special behalf, and Maximilian was sanguine enough to listen to the temptation. He faintly stipulated that the consent of England should be obtained, but was satisfied with Ferdinand's assurance that Henry would have no objection to a truce with France. Early in April 1514 a truce for a year was made between Louis XII., Maximilian, and Ferdinand. Henry found himself tricked by his father-in-law, and abandoned by the ally whom he had largely subsidised, and had greatly benefited.

It is no wonder that Henry was greatly angered at this result, and declared that he would trust no man any more. He had taken the measure of the good faith of European rulers, and had learned the futility of great undertakings for the general welfare. In truth, the difficulty of European politics always lies in the fact that the general welfare can only be promoted by the furtherance of particular interests, which threaten in their turn to become dangerous. The interests of the sixteenth century were purely dynastic interests, and seem trivial and unworthy. We are not, however, justi-fied in inferring that dynastic interests, because they are concerned with small arrangements, are in their nature more selfish or more iniquitous than interests which clothe themselves in more fair-sounding phrases Their selfishness is more apparent ; it does not follow that it is less profound.

However that may be, the desertion of Maximilian and Ferdinand put a stop to Henry's warlike projects, and restored England to peace. Henry had had enough of fighting other people's battles. He was willing to pursue his own course by the means which others used, and trust henceforth to the bloodless battles of diplomacy. In this new field Wolsey was the English champion, and for the next sixteen years the history of England is the history of Wolsey's achievements.

Wolsey's services in the campaign of 1513 gave him a firm hold of the king's favour, and secured for him large rewards. As he was an ecclesiastic his salary was paid out of the revenues of the Church. When Tournai became an English possession its bishopric was conferred on Wolsey, and on a vacancy in the bishopric of Lincoln in the beginning of 1514 that see was given him in addition. How the offices of the Church were in those days used as rewards for service to the State may be seen by the fact that the English representative in Rome was the Archbishop of York, Thomas Bainbridge, who lived as Cardinal in the Papal Court. Moreover, an Italian, Silvestro de' Gigli, held the bishopric of Worcester, though he lived habitually in Rome, and devoted his energies to the furtherance of the interests of England. In July 1514 Cardinal Bainbridge died in Rome, poisoned by one of his servants. The Bishop of Worcester was suspected of being privy to the deed for the purpose of removing out of the way a troublesome rival. It would seem, however, that the murder was prompted by vengeful feelings and the desire to hide peculations. The charge against the Bishop of Worcester was investigated by the Pope, and he was acquitted; but the story gives a poor picture of morality and security of life at Rome. On the death of Bainbridge the vacant archbishopric of York was also conferred on Wolsey, who was now enriched by the revenues of three sees, and was clearly marked out as the foremost man in England.

He rose to this position solely by the king's favour, as the king alone chose his own ministers and counsellors, and there existed no external pressure which could influence his decisions. The Wars of the Roses had seen the downfall of the baronial power, and Henry VII. had accustomed men to see affairs managed almost entirely by a new class of officials. The ministers and counsellors of Henry VIII. were chosen from a desire to balance the old and the new system. The remnants of the baronial party were associated with officials, that they might be assimilated into the same class. The Duke of Norfolk, as the greatest nobleman in England, was powerful, and was jealous of the men with whom he found himself called upon to work. Charles Brandon, Duke of Suffolk, was the personal friend of the king, and shared in his private more than in his public life. The Earl of Surrey had done good service at Flodden Field, and was a man of practical capacity. The other ministers were most of them ecclesiastics. Warham, Archbishop of Canterbury, was respected rather than trusted. Fox, Bishop of Winchester, was a capable and painstaking official. Ruthal, Bishop of Durham, was destitute of real insight, and was content to follow Wolsey's lead. Wolsey won his way by his political genius, his quickness, and his vast power of detailed work. He owed his position entirely to the king, and was responsible to him alone. The king consulted his Council only about such matters as he thought fit; foreign affairs were managed almost entirely according to his own will and pleasure.

The English have never been famous for diplomacy, and Wolsey was ill supplied with agents for his work. The English residents at foreign Courts were not men of mark or position. John Stile at the Court of Ferdinand, and Thomas Spinelly in Flanders seem to have been merchants carrying on their own business. With Maximilian was a more important man, Sir Richard Wingfield, a Suffolk knight, who was too self-satisfied and too dull-witted to understand Wolsey's schemes. For special work special agents had to be sent, who went unwillingly to a thankless and laborious task. They were ill paid and ill supported; but even here Wolsey knew how to choose the right men, and he managed to inspire them with his own zeal and tenacity of purpose. It is a striking proof of Wolsey's genius that he knew whom he could trust, and that his trust was never misplaced.

When Henry VIII. was smarting under his rebuff from Maximilian and Ferdinand, he concerted with Wolsey how he might avenge himself, and Wolsey devised his scheme in entire secrecy. Ferdinand and Maximilian had left England in the lurch by making a truce with France. Wolsey resolved to outdo them in their own lines. They had elected to maintain the existing condition of affairs by checking England's aspirations and lending a cold support to France. Wolsey resolved to turn France into a firm ally, that so England and France united might form a new combination, before which the schemes of Ferdinand would be powerless.

Wolsey luckily had the means of approaching Louis XII. without attracting attention. Amongst the prisoners taken in the Battle of the Spurs was the young Duke of Longueville, a favourite of the French king. He had been sent to London, to the sore disturbance of Queen Katharine, who, being a sensible woman, thought that the best thing to do with a prisoner was to confine him in the Tower. On Henry's return the Duke of Longueville was released, and amused himself at Court like any one else. Through him Wolsey opened up secret communications with Louis XII., whose domestic circumstances luckily gave a handle for Wolsey's designs. In January 1514 the French queen died; and although the widowed husband had reached the age of fifty-two, it was known that he was looking out for a young bride.

It has always been one of the most revolting features of dynastic politics that the private relationships of members of ruling families have been entirely determined by considerations of dynastic expediency. In the sixteenth century this was eminently the case. Alliances were family arrangements, and corresponded to motives of family aggrandisement rather than to national interests. They were sealed by marriages, they were broken by divorces. So great were the responsibilities of royalty that the private life of members of royal houses was entirely sunk in their official position. They were mere counters to be moved about the board at will, and disposed of according to the needs of family politics. Such a victim of circumstances was Henry VIII.'s younger sister, the Princess Mary, a bright and intelligent girl of seventeen. She was betrothed to Charles, Prince of Castile, and it had been arranged that the marriage should take place when he reached the age of fourteen The time was come for the fulfilment of the promise; but Ferdinand did not wish to see his troublesome grandson more closely united to England, which had shown such ambitious inclinations. Maximilian, the guardian of Charles, wavered between his desire to please Henry and Ferdinand, and invented one excuse after another for not proceeding with his grandson's marriage.

Wolsey allowed Maximilian to go on with his shifty talk, and was only too glad to see him fall into the trap. His negotiations with France were progressing, and the outward sign of the new alliance was to be the marriage of Mary to Louis XII. So secretly were the arrangements made that Europe was taken by surprise when, at the end of July, it was gradually known that the alliance between France and England was an accomplished fact. The marriage contract was soon signed, and in October Mary went to Abbeville, where she was met by her elderly husband.

The result of this clever diplomacy was to secure England the respect and envy of Europe. It was clear that henceforth England was a power which had to be reckoned with. Ferdinand was taught that he could no longer count on using his dutiful son-in-law as he thought most convenient to himself. Maximilian sadly reflected that if he needed English gold in the future he must show a little more dexterity in his game of playing fast and loose with everybody. Pope Leo X. was not over-pleased at seeing England develop a policy of her own, and looked coldly on Wolsey. After the death of Cardinal Bainbridge Henry wrote to the Pope and begged him to make Wolsey cardinal in his room. "Such are his merits," said the king, "that I esteem him above my dearest friends, and can do nothing of importance without him." Leo X. coldly replied that there were great difficulties in the way of creating a cardinal : the title, he reminded the king, was much sought after, and admitted its bearer to the highest rank : he must wait a more suitable time. It would seem that the Pope wished to have further guarantees of England's good-will, and hinted that Wolsey must give pledges of his good behaviour.

England did not long enjoy the diplomatic victory which Wolsey had won by his brilliant scheme of a French alliance. Henry still had a longing for military glory, with which Wolsey had little sympathy. He wished to revenge himself on his perfidious father-in-law, and proposed to Louis XII. an attack upon Navarre, and even thought of claiming a portion of the kingdom of Castile, as rightfully belonging to Queen Katharine. Whatever projects Henry may have had came to an end on the death of Louis on the 1st of January 1515. The elderly bridegroom, it was said, tried too well to humour the social disposition of his sprightly bride. He changed his manner of life, and kept late hours, till his health entirely gave way, and he sank under his well-meant efforts to renew the gallantry of youth.

CHAPTER III

THE death of Louis XII. was a severe blow to Wolsey. The French alliance was not popular in England, and was bitterly opposed by the Duke of Norfolk and the party of the old nobility, who saw with dislike the growing influence of Wolsey. They now had an opportunity of reversing his policy and securing his downfall. It required all Wolsey's sagacity to devise a means of solving the difficulties which the death of Louis created. The new king of France, Francis I., was aged twenty-one, and was as ambitious of distinction as was Henry. The treaty between France and England had not yet been carried out, and it would require much dexterity to modify its provisions. The kings of the sixteenth century were keen men of business, and never let money slip through their hands. The widowed Queen of France must, of course, return to England, but there were all sorts of questions about her dowry and the jewels which Louis had given her. Henry claimed that she should bring back with her everything to which any title could be urged: Francis I. wished to give up as

little as possible.   The two monarchs haggled like two
hucksters, and neither of them had any care of the
happiness or reputation of the young girl round whom
they bickered.   In the background stood Wolsey's
enemies, who saw that if they could create a rupture
between France and England Wolsey's influence would
be at an end.

In these dangerous conditions Wolsey had to seek an
ally in Charles Brandon, Duke of Suffolk, and had to
trust to his private knowledge of the character of Queen
Mary.   She had the strong will of the Tudors, and had
also their craving for admiration.   These two qualities
seem to have drawn her in opposite directions.   While
her marriage with Prince Charles was talked of she professed the greatest admiration for him, and gazed with
rapture on a very bad portrait of her intended husband.
But this did not prevent her from being attracted by
the personal fascinations of the Duke of Suffolk, as
Wolsey knew.   When he negotiated the French alliance
he had some difficulty in overcoming Mary's repugnance
to an old husband; but she viewed the proposal in a
business-like way, and was not indifferent to the position
of Queen of France.   She looked forward to a speedy
widowhood, and extracted from Henry a promise that,
if she undertook to marry for the first time to please
him, she might choose her second husband to please
herself.   When Mary was free the hopes of the Duke
of Suffolk revived, and Wolsey knowing this, chose
him as the best instrument for clearing away the difficulties raised by Francis I., and bringing back Mary
honourably to England.

Francis, on his side, used his knowledge of the current

rumour to extract from Mary her confidences about Suffolk, and with this knowledge approached Suffolk as a friend. By alternately encouraging Suffolk and terrifying Mary he turned Wolsey's ambassador into an anxious lover. Still Wolsey trusted that Suffolk would the more bestir himself to bring Mary back, and would make such terms with Francis as would commend his suit to Henry. But Wolsey's enemies led Henry to make exorbitant demands, which Francis met by redoubling his persecution of Mary. At last she asked Suffolk to marry her, which he did in secret. After this Francis was free from any further need of conciliating Henry, who must take back his sister on any terms, and Wolsey was left to appease Henry as best he could. In April Mary and Suffolk returned to England, and in May the luckless pair were publicly married. Wolsey manfully befriended Suffolk in this matter, but the calculations of his diplomacy were hopelessly upset by private feelings and the rashness of passion.

However, Mary received part of her dowry and some of her jewels. Francis I. had no wish to quarrel with England, but only to make the best terms for himself. He was bent upon gathering laurels in Italy, and on 5th April renewed the alliance between France and England. This time, however, the treaty was little more than a truce, and many questions were left untouched; no mention was made of the return of Tournai, and the question of Mary's jewels was left undecided. Francis I. counted on keeping England quiet by an alliance which he formed at the same time with Ferdinand, while he won over the Flemish counsellors of Prince Charles, who betrothed himself to the infant daughter of Louis XII., Renée, a child of four.

Thus he had cleared the way for an expedition to Italy, where he longed to claim for France the Duchy of Milan, that had been won and lost by Louis XII. In July he set out contentedly, knowing that Henry was powerless to interfere. He treated England with neglect, and gave Henry no information of his movements. England looked on with growing jealousy while Francis crossed the Alps and in September defeated the Swiss mercenaries who held Milan in the name of the last Sforza Duke. The battle of Marignano (14th September) was a splendid success for Francis, who there beat back the Swiss infantry, hitherto considered invincible in Europe. The star of France had risen, and Francis could look round with proud superiority.

The princes of Europe were alarmed beyond measure at the completeness of the French success. They had looked with equanimity at the preparations of Francis, because they expected that he would be delayed, or, if he attacked the Swiss, would be defeated. But his rapid march soon convinced men that he was in earnest, and especially excited the fear of Pope Leo X , whose ingenious policy of being secretly allied with everybody was disturbed by this display of unexpected vigour. The alarm of the Pope was useful to Wolsey. It awakened him to the need of making the English king his friend, and fulfilling his desire to have Wolsey created cardinal. Wolsey had not ceased, through his agent, the Bishop of Worcester, to urge this point upon the Pope, and when Francis was well advanced on his road to Milan the pleadings of Wolsey were irresistible. "If the King of England forsake the Pope," wrote Wolsey to the Bishop of Worcester, "he will be in greater danger on this day two years than ever was Pope Julius." Leo X. had no wish to run the risks which the impetuous Julius II. faced with unbroken spirit. He prepared to keep himself supplied with allies to protect him against all emergencies, and on 10th September nominated Wolsey cardinal sole, a special mark of favour, as cardinals were generally created in batches at intervals.

Wolsey's creation was not popular in the Roman Court. Cardinal Bainbridge had been overbearing in manner and hasty in temper, and the English were disliked for their outspokenness. England was regarded as a political upstart, and Wolsey was considered to be a fitting emblem of the country which he represented. Moreover, the attitude of England in ecclesiastical matters was not marked by that subservience which the Papacy wished to exact, and many doubted the expediency of exalting in ecclesiastical authority an English prelate of such far-reaching views as Wolsey was known to hold. An official of the Roman Court gives the following account of the current opinion :—

"Men say that an English Cardinal ought not to be created lightly, because the English behave themselves insolently in that dignity, as was shown in the case of Cardinal Bainbridge just dead. Moreover, as Wolsey is the intimate friend of the king, he will not be contented with the Cardinalate alone, but, as is the custom of these barbarians, will wish to have the office of legate over all England. If this be granted the influence of the Roman Court will be at an end ; if it be not granted the Cardinal will be the Pope's enemy and will favour France. But despite all this the Pope, in whose hands alone the matter was, created him Cardinal on the seventh of September."

This elevation of Wolsey was due to the strong expression of desire on the part of Henry, who further asked that legatine powers should be given to the new cardinal. This Leo refused for the present; he had done enough to induce Henry to enter into a secret league for the protection of the Church, which meant a convenient pretext for attacking Francis if he became too powerful in Italy. When this was arranged the red hat was sent to England, and its reception gave Wolsey an opportunity of displaying his love for magnificent ceremonial. On 17th November it was placed on his head by Archbishop Warham in Westminster Abbey.

Ceremonial, however splendid, was but an episode in Wolsey's diplomatic business. The news of the French victory at Marignano was so unpleasant that Henry VIII. for some time refused to believe it to be true. When at last it was impossible to doubt any longer, the necessity became urgent to put a spoke in the wheel of Francis I. England was not prepared to go to war with France without allies, and Wolsey developed his cleverness in attaining his ends by secret means. Nothing could be done by uniting with the cautious Ferdinand; but the flighty Maximilian was a more hopeful subject. The only troops that could be used against France were the German and Swiss mercenaries, men who made war a trade, and were trained and disciplined soldiers. The first means of injuring France was to prevent her from hiring Swiss soldiers, and the second was to induce Maximilian to undertake an

Italian expedition in his own interests. As regards the
Swiss, it was merely a matter of money, for they were
ready to sell themselves to the highest bidder. In like
manner it was easy to subsidise Maximilian, but it was
difficult to hold him to his promise and be sure that he
would spend the money on the right purpose. Wolsey,
however, resolved to try and use Maximilian; he offered
him the aid of a large contingent of the Swiss if he
would attack Milan. Knowing the delicacy of the
enterprise and the slipperiness of Maximilian, Wolsey
entrusted this matter to a man whose pertinacity had
been already tried,—Richard Pace, secretary of Cardinal
Bainbridge, who had stubbornly insisted on an investiga-
tion of the circumstances of his master's death, and had
annoyed the Roman Court by his watchful care of his
master's effects. Pace was sent to hire soldiers amongst
the Swiss, and Wolsey's ingenuity was sorely tried to
supply him with money secretly and safely.

The hindrances which beset Pace in carrying out his
instructions decorously were very many. Not the least
troublesome was the want of intelligence displayed by
Sir Robert Wingfield, the English envoy to Maximilian.
Wingfield belonged to the old school of English officials,
honest and industrious, but entirely incapable of *finesse.*
He did not understand what Pace was about; he could
not comprehend Wolsey's hints, but was a blind admirer
of Maximilian, and was made his tool in his efforts to
get the gold of England and do nothing in return. But
Pace was deaf to the entreaties of Maximilian and to
the lofty remonstrances of Wingfield. He raised 17,000
Swiss soldiers, who were to serve under their own
general, and whose pay was not to pass through Maxi

milian's hands. Maximilian was sorely disappointed at
this result, but led his troops to join the Swiss in an
attack on Milan. On 24th March 1516, the combined
army was a few miles from Milan, which was poorly
defended, and victory seemed secure. Suddenly Maximilian began to hesitate, and then drew off his forces
and retired. We can only guess at the motive of this
strange proceeding; perhaps he had never been in
earnest, and only meant to extract money from England.
When Pace refused to pay he probably negotiated with
Francis I., and obtained money from him. Anyhow his
withdrawal was fatal to the expedition. The Germans
at Brescia seized the money which was sent to Pace for
the payment of the Swiss. The Swiss in anger muti-
nied, and Pace was for some days thrown into prison.
Maximilian vaguely promised to return, but the Swiss
troops naturally disbanded. Such was Maximilian's
meanness that he threatened Pace, now deserted and
broken by disappointment, that if he did not advance
him money he would make peace with France. Pace,
afraid to run the risk, pledged Henry VIII. to pay
60,000 florins. All this time Wingfield was convinced
that it was Pace's ill-judged parsimony that had wrought
this disaster, and he continued to write in a strain of
superior wisdom to Wolsey. He even, at Maximilian's
bidding, forged Pace's name to receipts for money.
Never was diplomat in more hopeless plight than the
unlucky Pace.

Wolsey saw that his plan had failed, but he put a
good face upon his failure. Maximilian enjoyed the
advantage which consummate meanness always gives
for a moment. He put down the failure to niggardli-

ness in the supplies, and showed his goodwill towards
Henry by treating him to fantastic proposals.   If
Henry would only cross to Flanders with 6000 men,
Maximilian would meet him with his army, set him
up as Duke of Milan, and resign the Empire in his
favour.   This preposterous scheme did not for a moment
dazzle'the good sense of the English counsellors.   Pace,
in announcing it to Wolsey, pointed out that the Emperor
spoke without the consent of the Electors, that Maximilian was thoroughly untrustworthy, and that Henry
in such an enterprise might imperil his hold upon the
English Crown, "which," writes Pace with pardonable
pride, "is this day more esteemed than the Emperor's
crown and all his empire."   Henry was of the same
opinion; and Maximilian failed on this plea "to pluck
money from the king craftily."   Pace remained, and
jingled English money in Maximilian's ear, as a means
of preventing him from turning to France; but not a
penny was Maximilian allowed to touch, to Sir Robert
Wingfield's great annoyance.   Pace so far succeeded, that
when, in November 1516, Francis I. made an alliance
with the Swiss, five of the cantons stood aloof.   Pace
was rewarded for his labours and sufferings by being
made a secretary of state.   Sir Robert Wingfield received
a severe rebuke from the king, which sorely disturbed
his self-complacency.   But it is characteristic of Wolsey's
absence of personal feeling that Wingfield was not
recalled from his post.   Wolsey saw that he had been no
more foolish than most other Englishmen would have
been in his place.

Meanwhile a change had taken place in the affairs
of Europe which turned the attention of France and

England alike in a new direction. Ferdinand the Catholic died in January 1516, and the preponderance of France had so alarmed him that he laid aside his plan of dividing the power of the House of Austria by instituting his second grandson, Ferdinand, King of Spain. After the battle of Marignano he changed his will in favour of his eldest grandson, the Archduke Charles, who now added the Spanish kingdoms to his possession of the Netherlands. The young prince had just emancipated himself from the tutelage of Maximilian, but was under the influence of ministers who pursued a purely Flemish policy, and longed to give peace to the Netherlands by an alliance with France. England was connected with Flanders by commercial interests, and long negotiations had been conducted with the Flemish Government for a close alliance. But Charles's advisers were won over by France, and Charles himself was attracted by the hope of a French marriage. His position was difficult, as he was poor and helpless; he could not even go to take possession of the Spanish Crowns without help from one side or the other. Had he been older and wiser he would have seen that it was safer to accept the gold of Henry VIII., from whose future projects he had nothing to fear, rather than try and secure a precarious peace for the Netherlands by an alliance with France. However, Charles turned a cold ear to the English ambassadors, and his ministers secretly brought about a treaty with France, which was signed at Noyon in August 1516.

The Treaty of Noyon was a further rebuff to Wolsey, England was passed by in silence, and a tempting bait was laid to draw Maximilian also into the French alliance, and so leave England entirely without allies

Maximilian had been for some time at war with Venice about the possession of the towns of Brescia and Verona. The Treaty of Noyon provided that the Venetians should pay the Emperor 200,000 crowns and remain in possession of the disputed territory. Maximilian used this offer to put himself up to auction; he expressed his detestation of the peace of Noyon, but pleaded that unless Henry came to his help he would be driven by poverty to accept the proffered terms. Henry answered by a proposal that Maximilian should earn the price he fixed upon his services: let him come into the Netherlands, and work the overthrow of the unworthy ministers who gave such evil advice to their sovereign. Maximilian stipulated for the allowance which he was to receive for the expenses of a journey to the Netherlands, for which he began to make preparations. He raised all possible doubts and difficulties, and received all the money he could extract on any pretext from Henry VIII.; at last he secretly signed the Treaty of Noyon in December, and drew his payments from both parties so long as he could keep his game unsuspected.

But Wolsey was not so much deceived as Maximilian thought, and showed no discomfiture when Maximilian's shiftiness at length came to light. If Maximilian would not be faithful it was well that his untrustworthiness should be openly shown, and Francis I., who was watching his manœuvres, could not feel proud of his new ally. He knew what he had to expect from Maximilian when the 200,000 crowns were spent. The money that had been spent on Maximilian was not wasted if it gave him an encouragement to display his feebleness to the full.

So Henry maintained a dignified attitude, and showed no resentment. He received Maximilian's excuses with cold politeness, and waited for Francis I. to discover the futility of his new alliances. Maximilian was clearly of no account. Charles had gained all that he could gain from his League with France towards quieting the Netherlands; for his next step, a journey to Spain, he needed the help of England, and soon dropped his attitude of indifference. After thwarting England as much as he could, he was driven to beg for a loan to cover the expenses of his journey, and England showed no petty resentment for his past conduct. The loan was negotiated, Charles's ambassadors were honourably received, it was even proposed that he should visit Henry on his way. This honour Charles cautiously declined on the ground of ill health; but all the other marks of Henry's goodwill were accepted with gratitude, and in September 1517 Charles set out on his voyage to Spain, where he found enough to employ his energies for some time.

This conciliatory attitude of England was due to a perception that the time had come when simple opposition to France was no longer useful. England·had so far succeeded as to prevent the French ascendency from being complete; she had stemmed the current, had shown Francis I. the extent of her resources, and had displayed unexpected skill. Moreover, she had made it clear that neither she nor France could form a combination sufficiently powerful to enable the one to crush the other, and had given Francis I. a lesson as to the amount of fidelity he might expect from his allies When it was clear to both sides that there was no hope

for far-reaching schemes, it was natural for the two
powers to draw together, and seek a reasonable redress
for the grievances which immediately affected them.

Chief amongst these on the French side was the possession of Tournai by the English, glorious, no doubt,
as a trophy of English valour, but of very doubtful advantage to England. Negotiations about its restoration
were begun as early as March 1517, and were conducted
with profound secrecy. Of course Charles hoped to get
Tournai into his own hands, and did not wish it to be
restored to France. It was necessary to keep him in
ignorance of what was going on, and not till he had
sailed to Spain were there any rumours of what was
passing.

Wolsey and Henry VIII. deceived the ambassadors
of Charles and of Venice by their repeated professions
of hostility against France, and Charles's remonstrances
were answered by equivocations, so that he had no opportunity for interfering till the matter had been agreed
upon as part of a close alliance between England and
France. The negotiations for this purpose were long and
intricate, and form the masterpiece of Wolsey's diplomatic skill. They were made more difficult by the outbreak in England of a pestilence, the sweating sickness,
before which Henry fled from London and moved un-
easily from place to place. Wolsey was attacked by it
in June so seriously that his life was despaired of;
scarcely was he recovered when he suffered from a
second attack, and soon after went on a pilgrimage to
Walsingham to perform a vow and enjoy change of air.
But with this exception, he stuck manfully to his work
in London, where, beside his manifold duties in internal

administration, he directed the course of the negotiations with France.

In fact Wolsey alone was responsible for the change of policy indicated by the French alliance. He had thoroughly carried the king with him; but he was well aware that his course was likely to be exceedingly unpopular, and that on him would fall the blame of any failure. Henry did not even inform his Council of his plans. He knew that they would all have been opposed to such a sudden change of policy, which could only be justified in their eyes by its manifest advantage in the end. Wolsey was conscious that he must not only conclude an alliance with France, but must show beyond dispute a clear gain to England from so doing.

Wolsey's difficulties were somewhat lessened by the birth of an heir to the French Crown in February 1518. France could now offer, as a guarantee for her close alliance with England, a proposal of marriage between the Dauphin and Henry's only daughter Mary. Still the negotiations cautiously went on while Wolsey drove the hardest bargain that he could. They were not finished till September, when a numerous body of French nobles came on a splendid embassy to London. Never had such magnificence been seen in England before as that with which Henry VIII. received his new allies. Even the French nobles admitted that it was beyond their power to describe. Wolsey entertained the company at a sumptuous supper in his house at Westminster, "the like of which," says the Venetian envoy, "was never given by Cleopatra or Caligula, the whole banqueting hall being decorated with huge vases of gold and silver." After the banquet a band of mummers, wearing visors on their faces, entered and danced. There were twelve ladies and twelve gentle men, attended by twelve torch-bearers; all were clad alike "in fine green satin, all over covered with cloth of gold, undertied together with laces of gold." They danced for some time and then removed their masks, and the evening passed in mirth. Such were the festivities of the English Court, which Shakespeare has reproduced, accurately enough, in his play of *Henry VIII.*

But these Court festivities were only preliminary to the public ceremonies whereby Wolsey impressed the imagination of the people. The proclamation of the treaty and the marriage of the Princess Mary by proxy were both the occasions of splendid ceremonies in St Paul's Cathedral. The people were delighted by pageantry and good cheer; the opposition of old-fashioned politicians was overborne in the prevailing enthusiasm; and men spoke only of the triumph of a pacific policy which had achieved results such as warfare could not have won. Indeed, the advantages which England obtained were substantial. France bought back Tournai for 600,000 crowns, and entered into a close alliance with England, which cut it off from interference in the affairs of Scotland, which was included in the peace so long as it abstained from hostilities. But more important than this was the fact that Wolsey insisted on the alliance between France and England being made the basis of a universal peace. The Pope, the Emperor, the King of Spain, were all invited to join, and all complied with the invitation.

None of them, however, complied with goodwill, least of all Pope Leo X., whose claim to be the official pacifier of Europe was rudely set aside by the audacious action of Wolsey. Leo hoped that the bestowal of a cardinal's hat had established a hold on Wolsey's gratitude; but he soon found that he was mistaken, and that his cunning was no match for Wolsey's force. No sooner had Wolsey obtained the cardinalate than he pressed for the further dignity of papal legate in England. Not unnaturally Leo refused to endow with such an office a minister already so powerful as to be almost independent; but Wolsey made him pay for his refusal. Leo wanted money, and the pressure of the Turk on Southern Europe lent a colour to his demand of clerical taxation for the purposes of a crusade. In 1517 he sent out legates to the chief kings of Christendom; but Henry refused to admit Cardinal Campeggio, saying that "it was not the rule of this realm to admit legates *à latere.*" Then Wolsey intervened and suggested that Campeggio might come if he would exercise no exceptional powers, and if his dignity were shared by himself. Leo was forced to yield, and Campeggio's arrival was made the occasion of stately ceremonies which redounded to Wolsey's glorification. Campeggio got little for the crusade, but served to grace the festivities of the French alliance, and afterwards to convey the Pope's adhesion to the universal peace. Wolsey had taken matters out of the Pope's hand, and Leo was driven to follow his lead with what grace he could muster. Perhaps as he sighed over his discomfiture he consoled himself with the thought that the new peace would not last much longer than those previously made : if he did, he was right in his opinion.

CHAPTER IV

THE object of Wolsey's foreign policy had been attained by the universal peace of 1518 England had been set up as the mediator in the politics of Europe. The old claims of the empire and the papacy had passed away in the conflict of national and dynastic interests, in which papacy and empire were alike involved. England, by virtue of its insular position, was practically outside the objects of immediate ambition which distracted its Continental neighbours; but England's commercial interests made her desirous of influence, and Henry VIII. was bent upon being an important personage. It was Wolsey's object to gratify the king at the least expense to the country, and so long as the king could be exalted by peaceful means, the good of England was certainly promoted at the same time. The position of England as the pacifier of Europe was one well qualified to develop a national consciousness of great duties to perform; and it may be doubted if a country is ever great unless it has a clear consciousness of some great mission.

Wolsey's policy had been skilful, and the results

which he had obtained were glorious; but it was difficult to maintain the position which he had won.   It was
one thing to proclaim a peace; it was another to contrive
that peace should be kept.   One important question
was looming in the distance when Wolsey's peace was
signed,—the succession to the empire on Maximilian's
death.   Unfortunately this question came rapidly forward for decision, as Maximilian died suddenly on
12th January 1519, and the politicians of Europe waited
breathlessly to see who would be chosen as his successor.

The election to the empire rested with the seven
electors, the chief princes of Germany; but if they had
been minded on this occasion to exercise freely their right,
it would have been difficult for them to do so.   The empire
had for a century been with the house of Austria, and Maximilian had schemed eagerly that it should pass to his
grandson Charles.   It is true that Charles was already
King of Spain, Lord of the Netherlands, and King of
Naples and Sicily, so that it seemed dangerous to increase
still further his great dominions.   But Charles urged his
claim, and his great rival, Francis I. of France, entered
the lists against him.   Strange as it may seem that a
French king should aspire to rule over Germany, Francis
I. could urge that he was almost as closely connected
with Germany as was Charles, whose interests were
bound up with those of Spain and the Netherlands.   In
the face of these two competitors, it was hard for the
electors to find a candidate of a humbler sort who would
venture to draw upon himself the wrath of their disappointment.   Moreover, the task of ruling Germany
was not such as to attract a small prince.   The Turks
were threatening its borders, and a strong man was

needed to deal with many pressing problems of its government. The electors, however, were scarcely guilty of any patriotic considerations ; they quietly put up their votes for auction between Francis and Charles, and deferred a choice as long as they could.

Both competitors turned for help to their allies, the Pope and the King of England, who found themselves greatly perplexed Leo X. did not wish to see French influence increased, as France was a dangerous neighbour in Italy ; nor did he wish to see the empire and the kingdom of Naples both held by the same man, for that was against the immemorial policy of the Papacy. So Leo intrigued and prevaricated to such an extent that it is almost impossible to determine what he was aiming at He managed, however, to throw hindrances in Wolsey's path, though we cannot be sure that he intended to do so.

Wolsey's plan of action was clear, though it was not dignified. He wished to preserve England's mediating attitude and give offence to no one ; consequently, he secretly promised his help both to Charles and Francis, and tried to arrange that each should be ignorant of his promises to the other. All went well till Leo, in his diplomatic divagations, commissioned his legate to suggest to Henry VIII. that it might be possible, after all, to find some third candidate for the empire, and that he was ready to try and put off the election for that purpose, if Henry agreed. Henry seems to have considered this as a hint from the Pope to become a candidate himself. He remembered that Maximilian had offered to resign the empire in his favour, but he forgot the sufficient reasons which had led him to

dismiss the proposal as fantastic and absurd. His
vanity was rather tickled with the notion of rivalling
Charles and Francis, and he thought that if the Pope
were on his side, his chances would be as good as theirs.

We can only guess at Wolsey's dismay when his
master laid this project before him. Whatever Wolsey
thought, he knew that it was useless to offer any opposition. However much he might be able to influence the
king's opinions in the making, he knew that he must
execute them when they were made. If Henry
had made up his mind to become a candidate for the
empire, a candidate he must be. All that could be done
was to prevent his determination from being hopelessly
disastrous. So Wolsey pointed out that great as were
the advantages to be obtained by gaining the empire,
there were dangers in being an unsuccessful candidate.
It was necessary first to make sure of the Pope, and then
to prosecute Henry's candidature by fair and honourable
means. Francis was spending money lavishly to win
supporters to his side; and Charles was reluctantly compelled to follow his example lest he should be outbid.
It would be unwise for Henry to squander his money
and simply raise the market price of the votes. Let
him make it clear to the greedy Germans that they
would not see the colour of England's money till the
English king had been really elected.

So Wolsey sent the most cautious instructions to his
agent in Rome to see if the Pope would take the responsibility of urging Henry to become a candidate;
but Leo was too cautious, and affected not to understand the hint. Then in May, Pace, who was now the king's
secretary, was sent to Germany to sound the electors

with equal care. He was to approach the electors who were on Francis's side, as though Henry were in favour of Francis, and was to act similarly to those who were in favour of Charles; then he was to hint cautiously that it might be well to choose some one more closely connected with Germany, and if they showed any acquiescence, was to suggest that Henry was "of the German tongue," and then was to sing his praises. Probably both Pace and Wolsey knew that it was too late to do anything serious. Pace reported that the money of France and Spain was flowing on all sides, and was of opinion that the empire was "the dearest merchandise that ever was sold," and would prove "the worst that ever was bought to him that shall obtain it." Yet still he professed to have hopes, and even asked for money to enter the lists of corruption. But this was needless, as the election at last proceeded quickly. The Pope came round to the side of Charles as being the least of two evils, and Charles was elected on 28th June.

Thus Wolsey succeeded in satisfying his master's demands without committing England to any breach with either of her allies. Henry VIII. could scarcely be gratified at the part that he had played, but Wolsey could convince him that he had tried his best, and that at any rate no harm had been done. Though Henry's proceedings were known to Francis and Charles, there ·was nothing at which they could take offence. Henry had behaved with duplicity, but that was only to be expected in those days; he had not pronounced himself strongly against either. The ill-will that had long been simmering between Charles V. and Francis I. had risen to the surface, and the long rivalry between the two monarchs was now declared. Each looked for allies, and the most important ally was England. Each had hopes of winning over the English king, and Wolsey wished to keep alive, without satisfying, the hopes of both, and so establish still more securely the power of England as holding the balance of the peace of Europe.

Wolsey's conduct in this matter throws much light on his relations to the king, and the method by which he retained his influence and managed to carry out his own designs. He appreciated the truth that a statesman must lead while seeming to follow—a truth which applies equally to all forms of government. Wolsey was responsible to no one but the king, and so had a better opportunity than has a statesman who serves a democracy to obtain permission to carry out a consecutive policy. But, on the other hand, he was more liable to be thwarted and interrupted in matters of detail by the interference of a superior. Wolsey's far-seeing policy was endangered by the king's vanity and obstinacy; he could not ask for time to justify his own wisdom, but was forced to obey. Yet even then he would not abandon his own position and set himself to minimise the inconvenience. It is impossible to know how often Wolsey was at other times obliged to give way to the king and adopt the second-best course; but in this case we find clear indications of the process. When he was driven from his course, he contrived that the deviation should be as unimportant as possible.

Wolsey's task of maintaining peace by English mediation was beset with difficulties now that the breach between Francis I. and Charles V. was clearly made. It was necessary for England to be friendly to both, and

not to be drawn by its friendliness towards either to
offend the other   In the matter of the imperial election
English influence had been somewhat on the side of
Charles, and Francis was now the one who needed
propitiation.   The treaty with France had provided for
a personal interview between the two kings, and Francis
was anxious that it should take place at once.   For
this purpose he strove to win the good offices of
Wolsey.   He assured him that in case of a papal election
he could command fourteen votes which should be given
in his favour.   Moreover, he conferred on him a signal
mark of his confidence by nominating him his plenipo-
tentiary for the arrangements about the forthcoming
interview.   By this all difficulties were removed, and
Wolsey stood forward before the eyes of Europe as the
accredited representative of the kings of England and
France at the same time.   It is no wonder that men
marvelled at such an unheard-of position for an English
subject.

But nothing that Francis had to give could turn
Wolsey away from his own path.   No sooner did he
know that the French interview was agreed upon than
he suggested to Charles that it would be well for
him also to have a meeting with the English king.   The
proposal was eagerly accepted, and Wolsey conducted
the negotiations about both interviews side by side.
Rarely did two meetings cause such a flow of ink and
raise so many knotty points.   At last it was agreed that
Charles should visit Henry in England in an informal
way before the French interview took place.   It was
difficult to induce the punctilious Spaniards to give
way to Wolsey's requirements.   It was a hard thing for

one who bore the high-sounding title of Emperor to agree
to visit a King of England on his own terms. But
Wolsey was resolute that everything should be done in
such a way as to give France the least cause of complaint. When the Spanish envoys objected to his
arrangements or proposed alterations, he brought them
to their bearings by saying, "Very well; then do not do it
and begone." They were made to feel their dependence
on himself. The interview was of their seeking, and must
be held on terms which he proposed, or not at all. This,
no doubt, was felt to be very haughty conduct on
Wolsey's part; but he had set on foot the scheme of
this double interview, by which Henry was to be
glorified and England's mediatorial position assured. It
was his business to see that his plan succeeded. So he
turned a deaf ear to the offers of the Spanish ambassadors. He was not to be moved by the promise of
ecclesiastical revenues in Spain. Even when the influence
of Spain was proffered to secure his election to the
Papacy, he coldly refused.

It has been said that Wolsey was open to bribes,
and his seemingly tortuous policy has been accounted
for by the supposition that he inclined to the side which
promised him most. This, however, is an entire mistake.
Wolsey went his own way; but at the same time he did
not disregard his personal profit. He was too great a
man to be bribed; but his greatness entailed magnificence, and magnificence is expensive. He regarded it as
natural that sovereigns who threw work upon his
shoulders should make some recognition of his labours.
This was the custom of the time; and Wolsey was by no
means singular in receiving gifts from foreign kings

The chief lords of Henry's Court received pensions from
the King of France; and the lords of the French
Court were similarly rewarded by Henry. This was
merely a complimentary custom, and was open and
avowed Wolsey received a pension from Francis I,
and a further sum as compensation for the bishopric of
Tournai, which he resigned when Tournai was returned
to France.   In like manner, Charles V. rewarded him
by a Spanish bishopric; but Wolsey declined the office
of bishop, and preferred to receive a fixed pension
secured on the revenues of the see.   This iniquitous
arrangement was carried out with the Pope's consent;
and such like arrangements were by no means rare.
They were the natural result of the excessive wealth of
the Church, which was diverted to the royal uses by a
series of fictions, more or less barefaced, but all tending
to the weakening of the ecclesiastical organisation. Still
the fact remains that Wolsey thought no shame of
receiving pensions from Francis and Charles alike; but
there was nothing secret nor extraordinary in this.
Wolsey regarded it as only obvious that his statesmanship should be rewarded by those for whom it was
exercised; but the Emperor and the King of France
never hoped that by these pensions they would attach
Wolsey to their side.   The promise by which they tried
to win him was the promise of the Papacy; and to this
Wolsey turned a deaf ear.   " He is seven times more
powerful than the Pope," wrote the Venetian ambassador;
and perhaps Wolsey himself at this time was of the
same opinion.

Meanwhile Francis was annoyed when he heard of
these dealings with Charles, and tried to counteract

them by pressing for an early date of his meeting with
Henry VIII. It is amazing to find how large a part
domestic events were made to play in these matters of
high policy when occasion needed. Francis urged that
he was very anxious for his queen to be present to
welcome Katharine; but she was expecting her confine-
ment, and if the interview did not take place soon she
would be unable to appear. Wolsey replied with equal
concern for family affairs, that the Emperor was anxious
to visit his aunt, whom he had never seen, and Henry
could not be so churlish as to refuse a visit from
his wife's relative. Katharine, on her side, was overjoyed at this renewal of intimacy with the Spanish
Court, to whose interests she was strongly attached, and
tried to prevent the understanding with France, by
declaring that she could not possibly have her dresses
ready under three months. In her dislike of the French
alliance Queen Katharine expressed the popular sentiment. The people had long regarded France as the
natural enemy of England, and were slow to give up
their prejudices. The nobles grew more and more discontented with Wolsey's policy, which they did not care
to understand. They only saw that their expectations
of a return to power were utterly disappointed; Wolsey,
backed by officials such as Pace, was all-powerful, and
they were disregarded. Wolsey was working absolutely
single-handed. It is a remarkable proof of his skill that
he was able to draw the king to follow him unhesitatingly, at the sacrifice of his personal popularity, and in
spite of the representations of those who were immediately around him.

Moreover, Wolsey, in his capacity of representative

of the Kings of England and France, had in his hands
the entire management of all concerning the coming
interview.   He fixed the place with due regard to the
honour of England, almost on English soil.   The
English king was not to lodge outside his own territory
of Calais ; the spot appointed for the meeting was on
the meadows between Guisnes and Ardres, on the border-
land of the two kingdoms. Wolsey had to decide which of
the English nobles and gentry were to attend the king,
and had to assign to each his office and dignity.   The
king's retinue amounted to nearly 4000, and the queen's
was somewhat over 1000.   A very slight knowledge of
human nature will serve to show how many people
Wolsey must necessarily have offended.   If the ranks
of his enemies were large before, they must have increased enormously when his arrangements were made
known.

Still Wolsey was not daunted, and however much
every one, from Francis and Charles, felt aggrieved by his
proceedings, all had to obey ; and everything that took
place was due to Wolsey's will alone.   The interview
with Charles was simple.   On 26th May 1520 he landed
at Dover, and was met by Wolsey ; next morning Henry
rode to meet him and escort him to Canterbury, which
was his headquarters ; on the 29th Charles rode to
Sandwich, where he embarked for Flanders.   What
subjects the two monarchs discussed we can only dimly
guess.   Each promised to help the other if attacked by
France, and probably Henry undertook to bring about a
joint-conference of the three sovereigns to discuss their
common interests.   The importance of the meeting lay
in its display of friendliness ; in the warning which it gave

to France that she was not to count upon the exclusive possession of England's goodwill.

No sooner was the Emperor gone than Henry embarked for Calais, and arrived at Guisnes on 4th June. We need not describe again the "Field of the Cloth of Gold," to furnish which the art of the Renaissance was used to deck medieval pageantry. It is enough to say that stately palaces of wood clothed the barren stretch of flat meadows, and that every ornament which man's imagination could devise was employed to lend splendour to the scene. No doubt it was barbaric, wasteful, and foolish; but men in those days loved the sight of magnificence, and the display was as much for the enjoyment of countless spectators as for the self-glorification of those who were the main actors. In those days the solace of a poor man's life was the occasional enjoyment of a stately spectacle; and after all, splendour gives more pleasure to the lookers-on than to the personages of the show.

Most splendid among the glittering throng was the figure of Wolsey, who had to support the dignity of representative of both·kings, and spared no pains to do it to the full. But while the jousts went on, Wolsey was busy with diplomacy; there were many points relating to a good understanding between France and England, which he wished to arrange,—the projected marriage of the Dauphin with Mary of England, the payment due from France to England on several heads, the relations between France and Scotland and the like. More important than these was the reconciliation of Charles with Francis, which Wolsey pressed to the utmost of his persuasiveness, without, however, reaching

any definite conclusion. Charles was hovering on the
Flemish border, ready at a hint from Wolsey to join
the conference; but Wolsey could find no good reasons
for giving it, and when the festivities came to an end on
24th June, it might be doubted if much substantial good
had resulted from the interview. No doubt the French
and English fraternised, and swore friendship over their
cups, but tournaments were not the happiest means of
allaying feelings of rivalry, and the protestations of
friendship were little more than lip-deep. Yet Wolsey
cannot be blamed for being over-sanguine. It was at
least a worthy end that he had before him,—the removal
of long-standing hostility, the settlement of old disputes,
the union of two neighbouring nations by the assertion
of common aims and common interests. However we
may condemn the methods which Wolsey used, at least
we must admit that his end was in accordance with the
most enlightened views of modern statesmanship.

When Henry had taken leave of Francis, he
waited in Calais for the coming of Charles, whose visit
to England was understood to be merely preliminary
to further negotiations. Again Henry held the important position; he went to meet Charles at Grave-
lines, where he stayed for a night, and then escorted
Charles as his guest to Calais, where he stayed from
10th to 14th July. The result of the conference was a
formal treaty of alliance between the two sovereigns,
which Charles proposed to confirm by betrothing
himself to Henry's daughter Mary. As she was a
child of four years old, such an undertaking did not bind
him to much; but Mary was already betrothed to the
Dauphin, while Charles was also already betrothed to

Charlotte of France, so that the proposal aimed at a double breach of existing relationships and treaties. Henry listened to this scheme, which opened up the way for further negotiation, and the two monarchs parted with protestations of friendship. It was now the turn of Francis to hang about the place where Henry was holding conference with his rival, in hopes that he too might be invited to their discussions. He had to content himself with hearing that Henry rode a steed which he had presented to him, and that his face did not look so contented and cheerful as when he was on the meadows of Guisnes. In due time he received from Henry an account of what had passed between himself and the Emperor. Henry informed him of Charles's marriage projects, and of his proposal for an alliance against France, both of which Henry falsely said that he had rejected with holy horror.

Truly the records of diplomacy are dreary, and the results of all this display, this ingenious scheming, and this deceit seem ludicrously small. The upshot, however, was that Wolsey's ideas still remained dominant, and that the position which he had marked out for England was still maintained. He had been compelled to change the form of his policy, but its essence was unchanged. European affairs could no longer be directed by a universal peace under the guarantee of England; so Wolsey substituted for it a system of separate alliances with England, by which England exercised a mediating influence on the policy of the two monarchs, whose rivalry threatened a breach of European peace. He informed Francis of the schemes of Charles, that he might show him how much depended on English mediation

He so conducted matters that Charles and Francis
should both be aware that England could make advan-
tageous terms with either, that her interests did not
tend to one side rather than the other, that both should
be willing to secure her goodwill, and should shrink
from taking any step which would throw her on the
side of his adversary. It was a result worth achieving,
though the position was precarious, and required constant watchfulness to maintain.

CHAPTER V

THE most significant point in the mediatorial policy of Wolsey was the fact that it threw the Papacy entirely into the shade. What Wolsey was doing was the traditional business of the Pope, who could not openly gainsay a policy which he was bound to profess coincided with his own. So Leo X. followed Wolsey's lead of keeping on good terms with France and the Emperor alike; but Leo had no real wish for peace. He wished to gain something in Italy for the Medici, and nothing was to be gained while France and Spain suspended hostilities. Only in time of war could he hope to carry out his own plans by balancing one combatant against the other. Charles's ambassador was not wrong in saying that Leo hated Wolsey more than any other man; and Leo tried to upset his plans by drawing nearer to the imperial side.

It required very little to provoke war between Francis and Charles; either would begin the attack if the conditions were a little more favourable, or if he could secure an ally. But Charles was weak owing to the

want of unity of interest in his unwieldy dominions.
Germany was disturbed by the opinions of Luther
Spain was disturbed by a revolt of the cities against
long-standing misgovernment. Charles was not ready
for war, nor was Francis much better provided. His
coffers were empty through his lavish expenditure, and
his Government was not popular. Really, though both
wished for war, neither was prepared to be the aggressor;
both wanted the vantage of seeming to fight in self-
defence.

It was obvious that Charles had made a high bid
for the friendship of England when he offered himself
as the husband of the Princess Mary. Wolsey had taken
care that Francis was informed of this offer, which
necessarily led to a long negotiation with the imperial
Court. Really Charles's marriage projects were
rather complicated; he was betrothed to Charlotte of
France; he had made an offer for Mary of England; but
he wished to marry Isabella of Portugal for no loftier
reason than the superior attractions of her dowry. His
proposal for Mary of England was prompted by nothing
save the desire to have Henry as his ally against
France; if he could manage by fair promises to induce
Henry to go to war his purpose would be achieved,
and he could still go in quest of the Portuguese dower.
So when Tunstal, the Master of the Rolls, went as English
envoy to discuss the matter, Charles's Council raised all
sorts of difficulties. Let the English king join a league
with the Pope and the Emperor against France; then the
Pope would grant his dispensation, which was necessary,
owing to the relationship between Charles and Mary.
Tunstal was bidden by Wolsey to refuse such conditions.

England would not move until the marriage had been concluded, and would not join in any league with the Pope till his dispensation was in Henry's hand. The separate alliance of England and the Emperor must be put beyond doubt to England's satisfaction before anything else could be considered. Wolsey commissioned Tunstal to adopt a lofty tone. "It would be great folly," he says, "for this young prince, not being more surely settled in his dominions, and so ill-provided with treasure and good councillors, the Pope also being so brittle and variable, to be led into war for the pleasure of his ministers." Truly Wolsey thought he had taken the measure of those with whom he dealt, and spoke with sufficient plainness when occasion needed. But Charles's chancellor, Gattinara, a Piedmontese, who was rising into power, was as obstinate as Wolsey, and rejected the English proposals with equal scorn. "Your master," he said to Tunstal, "would have the Emperor break with France, but would keep himself free; he behaves like a man with two horses, one of which he rides, and leads the other by the hand." It was clear that nothing could be done, and Wolsey with some delight recalled Tunstal from his embassy. The closer alliance with the Emperor was at an end for the present; he had shown again that England would only forego her mediating position on her own terms.

At the same time he dealt an equal measure of rebuff to France. Before the conference at Guisnes Francis had done some work towards rebuilding the ruined walls of Ardres on the French frontier. After the conference the work was continued till England resented it as an unfriendly act. Francis was obliged to give way, and order the building to be stopped. Neither Francis nor Charles were allowed to presume on the complacency of England, nor use their alliance with her to further their own purposes.

The general aspect of affairs was so dubious that it was necessary for England to be prepared for any emergency, and first of all Scotland must be secured as far as possible. Since the fall of James IV. at Flodden Field, Scotland had been internally unquiet. Queen Margaret gave birth to a son a few months after her husband's death, and, to secure her position, took the unwise step of marrying the Earl of Angus. The enemies of Angus and the national party in Scotland joined together to demand that the Regency should be placed in firmer hands, and they summoned from France the Duke of Albany, a son of the second son of James III., who had been born in exile, and was French in all the traditions of his education. When Albany came to Scotland as Regent, Queen Margaret and Angus were so assailed that Margaret had to flee to England for refuge in 1515, leaving her son in Albany's care. She stayed in England till the middle of 1517, when she was allowed to return to Scotland on condition that she took no part in public affairs. About the same time Albany returned to France, somewhat weary of his Scottish charge. By his alliance with Francis Henry contrived that Albany should not return to Scotland; but he could not contrive to give his sister Margaret the political wisdom which was needed to draw England and Scotland nearer together. Margaret quarrelled with her husband Angus, and only added another element of discord to those which previously existed. The safest way for England to keep

Scotland helpless was to encourage forays on the Border. The Warden of the Western Marches, Lord Dacre of Naworth, was admirably adapted to work with Wolsey for this purpose. Without breaking the formal peace which existed between the two nations, he developed a savage and systematic warfare, waged in the shape of Border raids, which was purposely meant to devastate the Scottish frontier, so as to prevent a serious invasion from the Scottish side. Still Henry VIII. was most desirous to keep Scotland separate from France; but the truce with Scotland expired in November 1520. Wolsey would gladly have turned the truce into a perpetual peace; but Scotland still clung to its French alliance, and all that Wolsey could achieve was a prolongation of the truce till 1522. He did so, however, with the air of one who would have preferred war; and Francis I. was induced to urge the Scots to sue for peace, and accept as a favour what England was only too glad to grant.

At the same time an event occurred in England which showed in an unmistakable way the determination of Henry to go his own way and allow no man to question it. In April 1520 the Duke of Buckingham, one of the wealthiest of the English nobles, was imprisoned on an accusation of high treason. In May he was brought to trial before his peers, was found guilty, and was executed. The charges against him were trivial if true; the witnesses were members of his household who bore him a grudge. But the king heard their testimony in his Council, and committed the duke to the Tower. None of the nobles of England dared differ from their imperious master. If the king thought fit that Bucking ham should die, they would not run the risk of putting any obstacle in the way of the royal will. Trials for treason under Henry VIII. were mere formal acts of registration of a decision already formed.

The Duke of Buckingham, no doubt, was a weak and foolish man, and may have done and said many foolish things. He was in some sense justified in regarding himself as the nearest heir to the English throne if Henry left no children to succeed him. Henry had been married for many years, and as yet there was no surviving child save the Princess Mary. It was unwise to talk about the succession to the Crown after Henry's death; it was criminal to disturb the minds of Englishmen who had only so lately won the blessings of internal peace. If the Duke of Buckingham had really done so, he would not be undeserving of punishment; but the evidence against him was slight, and its source was suspicious. No doubt Buckingham was incautious, and made himself a mouthpiece of the discontent felt by the nobles at the French alliance and their own exclusion from affairs. No doubt he denounced Wolsey, who sent him a message that he might say what he liked against himself, but warned him to beware what he said against the king. It does not seem that Wolsey took any active part in the proceedings against the Duke, but he did not do anything to save him. The matter was the king's matter, and as such it was regarded by all. The nobles, who probably agreed with Buckingham's opinions, were unanimous in pronouncing his guilt; and the Duke of Norfolk, with tears streaming down his cheeks, condemned him to his doom. The mass of the people were indifferent to his fate, and were willing that the king should be sole judge of the precautions necessary for his safety, with which the internal peace and outward glory of England was entirely identified.   Charles and Francis stood aghast at Henry's strong measures, and were surprised that he could do things in such a high-handed manner with impunity.   If Henry intended to let the statesmen of Europe know that he was not to be diverted from his course by fear of causing disorders at home he thoroughly succeeded.   The death of Buckingham was a warning that those who crossed the king's path and hoped to thwart his plans by petulant opposition were playing a game which would only end in their own ruin.

Free from any fear of opposition at home, Wolsey could now give his attention to his difficult task abroad. Charles V. had been crowned at Aachen, and talked of an expedition to Rome to receive the imperial crown. Francis I. was preparing for a campaign to assert the French claims on Milan.   Meanwhile he wished to hamper Charles without openly breaking the peace. He stirred up a band of discontented barons to attack Luxembourg, and aided the claimant to the crown of Navarre to enter his inheritance.   War seemed now inevitable ; but Wolsey remained true to his principles,, and urged upon both kings that they should submit their differences to the mediation of England.   Charles was busied with the revolt of the Spanish towns, and was not unwilling to gain time.   After a show of reluctance he submitted to the English proposals ; but Francis, rejoicing in the prospect of success in Luxembourg and Navarre, refused on the ground that Charles was not in earnest.   Still Francis was afraid of incurring

England's hostility, and quailed before Wolsey's threat that if France refused mediation, England would be driven to side with the Emperor. In June 1521 he reluctantly assented to a conference to be held at Calais, over which Wolsey should preside, and decide between the pleas urged by representatives of the two hostile monarchs.

If Wolsey triumphed at having reached his goal, his triumph was of short duration. He might display himself as a mediator seeking to establish peace, but he knew that peace was well-nigh impossible. While the negotiations were in progress for the conference which was to resolve differences, events were tending to make war inevitable. When Wolsey began to broach his project, Francis was desirous of war and Charles was anxious to defer it; but Charles met with some success in obtaining promises of help from Germany in the Diet of Worms, and when that was over, he heard welcome news which reached him gradually from all sides. The revolt of the Spanish towns was dying away; the aggressors in Luxembourg had been repulsed; the troops of Spain had won signal successes in Navarre. His embarrassments were certainly disappearing on all sides. More than this, Pope Leo X., after long wavering, made up his mind to take a definite course. No doubt he was sorely vexed to find that the position which he hankered after was occupied by England; and if he were to step back into the politics of Europe, he could not defer a decision much longer. He had wavered between an alliance with France and Venice on the one side, or with the Emperor on the other. The movement of Luther in Germany had been one of the questions for

settlement in the Diet of Worms, and Luther had been
silenced for a time.   Leo awoke in some degree to
the gravity of the situation, and saw the advantage of
making common cause with Charles, whose help in
Germany was needful.   Accordingly he made a secret
treaty with the Emperor for mutual defence, and was
anxious to draw England to the same side.   The
religious question was beginning to be of importance, and Francis I. was regarded as a favourer of
heretics, whereas Henry VIII. was strictly orthodox,
was busy in suppressing Lutheran opinions at home,
and was preparing his book which should confute Luther
for ever.

Another circumstance also greatly affected the attitude of Charles, the death of his minister Chièvres, who
had been his tutor in his youth, and continued to
exercise great influence over his actions.   Charles
was cold, reserved; and ill-adapted to make friends.
It was natural that one whom he had trusted from
his boyhood should sway his policy at the first.
Chièvres was a Burgundian, whose life had been spent
in saving Burgundy from French aggression, and the
continuance of this watchful care was his chief object till
the last.   His first thought was for Burgundy, and to
protect that he wished for peace with France and opposed
an adventurous policy.   On his death in May 1521
Charles V. entered on a new course of action.   He felt
himself for the first time his own master, and took his
responsibilities upon himself.   He seems to have admitted to himself that the advice of Chievres had not
always been wise, and he never allowed another minister
to gain the influence Chièvres had possessed. He contented

himself with officials who might each represent some part of his dominions, and whose advice he used in turns, but none of whom could claim to direct his policy as a whole.

Chief of these officials was a Savoyard, Mercurino della Gattinara, whose diplomatic skill was now of great service to the Emperor. Gattinara was a man devoted to his master's interests, and equal to Wolsey in resoluteness and pertinacity. Hitherto Wolsey had had the strongest will amongst the statesmen of Europe, and had reaped all the advantages of his strength. In Gattinara he met with an opponent who was in many ways his match. It is true that Gattinara had not Wolsey's genius, and was not capable of Wolsey's far-reaching schemes; but he had a keen eye to the interests of the moment, and could neither be baffled by *finesse* nor overborne by menaces. His was the hand that first checked Wolsey's victorious career.

So it was that through a combination of causes the prospects of peace suddenly darkened just as Wolsey was preparing to stand forward as the mediator of Europe. Doubtless he hoped, when first he put forward the project of a conference, that it might be the means of restoring his original design of 1518, a European peace under the guarantee of England. Since that had broken down he had been striving to maintain England's influence by separate alliances; he hoped in the conference to use this position in the interests of peace. But first of all the alliance with the Emperor must be made closer, and the Emperor showed signs of demanding that this closer alliance should be purchased by a breach with France. If war was inevitable, England had most to gain by an alliance with Charles, to whom its friendship could offer substantial advantages, as England, in case of war, could secure to Charles the means of communicating between the Netherlands and Spain, which would be cut off if France were hostile and the Channel were barred by English ships. Moreover the prospect of a marriage between Charles and the Princess Mary was naturally gratifying to Henry; while English industry would suffer from any breach of trading relations with the Netherlands, and the notion of war with France was still popular with the English.

So Wolsey started for Calais at the beginning of August with the intention of strengthening England's alliance with the Emperor, that thereby England's influence might be more powerful. Charles on the other hand was resolved on war; he did not wish for peace by England's mediation, but he wished to draw England definitely into the league between himself and the Pope against France. Wolsey knew that much depended on his own cleverness, and nerved himself for the greatest caution, as Francis was beginning to be suspicious of the preparations of Charles, and the attitude of affairs was not promising for a pacific mediation.

This became obvious at the first interview of Wolsey with the imperial envoys, foremost amongst whom was Gattinara. They were commissioned to treat about the marriage of Charles with the Princess Mary, and about a secret undertaking for war against France ; but their instructions contained nothing tending to peace. The French envoys were more pacific, as war was not popular in France.

On 7th August the conference was opened under
Wolsey's presidency; but Gattinara did nothing save
dwell upon the grievances of his master against France;
he maintained that France had been the aggressor in
breaking the existing treaty; he had no powers to
negotiate peace or even a truce, but demanded England's
help, which had been promised to the party first aggrieved.
The French retorted in the same strain, but it was clear
that they were not averse to peace, and were willing
to trust to Wolsey's mediation. Wolsey saw that he
could make little out of Gattinara. He intended to visit
the Emperor, who had come to Bruges for the purpose,
as soon as he had settled with the imperial envoys the
preliminaries of .an alliance; now he saw that the
only hope of continuing the conference lay in winning
from Charles better terms than the stubborn Gattinara
would concede. So he begged the French envoys to
remain in Calais while he visited the Emperor and
arranged with him personally for a truce. As the
French were desirous of peace, they consented.

On 16th August Wolsey entered Bruges in royal
state, with a retinue of 1000 horsemen. Charles came
to the city gate to meet him, and received him almost
as an equal. Wolsey did not dismount from his
horse, but received Charles's embrace seated. He was
given rooms in Charles's palace, and the next day at
church Charles sat by Wolsey's side and shared the same
kneeling stool with him. Their private conferences
dealt solely with the accord between England and the
Emperor. Wolsey saw that it was useless to urge
directly the cause of peace, and trusted to use for this
purpose the advantages which his alliance would give.

He succeeded, however, in considerably modifying the
terms which had been first proposed. He diminished
the amount of dowry which Mary was to receive on her
marriage, and put off her voyage to the Emperor till she
should reach the age of twelve, instead of seven, which
was first demanded. Similarly he put off the period
when England should declare war against France till
the spring of 1523, though he agreed that if war
was being waged between Francis and Charles in
November, England should send some help to Charles.
Thus he still preserved England's freedom of action, and
deferred a rupture with France. Every one thought that
many things might happen in the next few months, and
that England was pledged to little. Further, Wolsey
guarded the pecuniary interests of Henry by insist-
ing that if France ceased to pay its instalments for the
purchase of Tournai, the Emperor should make good
the loss. He also stipulated that the treaty should be
kept a profound secret, so that the proceedings of the
conference should still go on.

Wolsey was impressed by Charles, and gave a true
description of his character to Henry: "For his age
he is very wise and understanding his affairs, right
cold and temperate in speech, with assured manner,
couching his words right well and to good purpose when
he doth speak." We do not know what was Charles's
private opinion of Wolsey. He can scarcely have
relished Wolsey's lofty manner, for Wolsey bore himself
with all the dignity of a representative of his king.
Thus, the King of Denmark, Charles's brother-in-law, was
in Bruges, and sought an interview with Wolsey, who
answered that it was unbecoming for him to receive in

his chamber any king to whom he was not commissioned; if the King of Denmark wished to speak with
him, let him meet him, as though by accident, in the
garden of the palace.

When the provisions of the treaty had been drafted,
Wolsey set out for Calais on 26th August, and was
honourably escorted out of Bruges by the Emperor himself. On his return the business of the conference began,
and was dragged on through three weary months. The
imperial envoys naturally saw nothing to be gained by
the conference except keeping open the quarrel with
France till November, when Henry was bound to
send help to the Emperor if peace were not made.
Wolsey remained true to his two principles : care for
English interests, and a desire for peace. He secured
protection for the fishery of the Channel in case of war,
and he cautiously strove to lead up both parties to see their
advantage in making a truce if they could not agree
upon a peace. It was inevitable that these endeavours
should bring on Wolsey the suspicions of both. The
French guessed something of the secret treaty from the
warlike appearance which England began to assume, and
cried out that they were being deceived. The imperial
envoys could not understand how one who had just
signed a treaty with their master, could throw obstacles
in their way and pursue a mediating policy of his own.
Really both sides were only engaged in gaining time,
and their attention was more fixed upon events in the
field than on any serious project of agreement.

When in the middle of September the French arms
won some successes, Gattinara showed himself inclined to
negotiate for a truce. The conference, which hitherto

had been merely illusory, suddenly became real, and
Wolsey's wisdom in bargaining that England should
not declare war against France till the spring of 1523
became apparent. He could urge on Gattinara that it
would be wise to agree to a truce till that period was
reached; then all would be straightforward. So Wolsey adjourned the public sittings of the conference, and
negotiated privately with the two parties. The French
saw in a year's truce only a means of allowing the Emperor to prepare for war, and demanded a substantial
truce for ten years. Wolsey used all his skill to
bring about an agreement, and induced Gattinara to
accept a truce for eighteen months, and the French
to reduce their demands to four years. But Charles
raised a new difficulty, and claimed that all conquests
made in the war should be given up. The only conquest was Fontarabia, on the border of Navarre, which
was still occupied by the French. Francis not unnaturally declined to part with it solely to obtain a
brief truce, as Charles had no equivalent to restore.
Wolsey used every argument to induce the Emperor
to withdraw his claim; but he was obstinate, and
the conference came to an end. It is true that Wolsey
tried to keep up appearances by concluding a truce for
a month, that the Emperor might go to Spain and consult his subjects about the surrender of Fontarabia.

So Wolsey departed from Calais on 25th November,
disappointed and worn out. As he wrote himself, "I
have been so sore tempested in mind by the untowardness
of the chancellors and orators on every side, putting so
many difficulties and obstacles to condescend to any
reasonable conditions of truce and abstinence of war,

that night nor day I could have no quietness nor rest."
There is no doubt that Wolsey wrote what he felt. He
had laboured hard for peace, and had failed. If he
hoped that the labours of the conference might still be
continued by his diplomacy in England, that hope was
destroyed before he reached London. On 1st December
the imperial troops captured Tournai, which they had
been for some time besieging, and news came from Italy
that Milan also had fallen before the forces of the
Emperor and the Pope. Charles had seemed to Wolsey
unreasonable in his obstinacy. He had refused a truce
which he had every motive of prudence for welcoming ;
and now events proved that he was justified. Not
only had Francis been foiled in his attempts to embarrass his rival, but success had followed the first steps
which Charles had taken to retaliate. The time for
diplomacy was past, and the quarrel must be decided by
the sword.

So Wolsey saw his great designs overthrown. He
was a peace minister because he knew that England
had nothing to gain from war. He had striven to keep
the peace of Europe by means of England's mediation,
and his efforts had been so far successful as to give
England the first place in the counsels of Europe. But
Wolsey hoped more from diplomacy than diplomacy
could do. Advice and influence can do something to
check the outbreak of war when war is not very seriously designed ; but in proportion as great interests are
concerned, attempts at mediation are useless unless they
are backed by force. England was not prepared for
war, and had no troops by whom she could pretend to
enforce her counsels. When the two rival powers began

to be in earnest, they admitted England's mediation only as a means of involving her in their quarrel. Wolsey was only the first of a long series of English ministers who have met with the same disappointment from the same reason. England in Wolsey's days had the same sort of interest in the affairs of the Continent as she has had ever since. Wolsey first taught her to develop that interest by pacific counsels, and so long as that has been possible, England has been powerful. But when a crisis comes England has ever been slow to recognise its inevitableness; and her habit of hoping against hope for peace has placed her in an undignified attitude for a time, has drawn upon her reproaches for duplicity, and has involved her in war against her will.

This was now the net result of Wolsey's endeavours, a result which he clearly perceived. His efforts of mediation at Calais had been entirely his own, and he could confide to no one his regret and his disappointment. Henry was resolved on war when Wolsey first set forth, and if Wolsey had succeeded in making a truce, the credit would have been entirely his own. He allowed Henry to think that the conference at Calais was merely a pretext to gain time for military preparations; if a truce had been made he would have put it down to the force of circumstances; as his efforts for a truce had failed, he could take credit that he had done all in his power to establish the king's reputation throughout Christendom, and had fixed the blame on those who would not follow his advice. It is a mark of Wolsey's conspicuous skill that he never forgot his actual position, and never was so entirely absorbed in his own plans as not to leave himself a ready means for retreat. His schemes had failed; but he could still take credit for having furthered other ends which were contrary to his own. Henry was well contented with the results of Wolsey's mission, and showed his satisfaction in the customary way of increasing Wolsey's revenues at the expense of the Church. The death was announced of the Abbot of St. Albans, and the king, in answer to Wolsey's request, ordered the monks to take Wolsey for their abbot, saying, " My lord cardinal has sustained many charges in this his voyage, and hath expended £10,000." So kings were served, and so they recompensed their servants.

CHAPTER VI

THE IMPERIAL ALLIANCE

1521-1523

THE failure of Wolsey's plans was due to the diplomacy of Gattinara and to the obstinacy of Charles V., who showed at the end of the negotiations at Calais an unexpected readiness to appreciate his obligations towards his dominions as a whole, by refusing to abandon Fontarabia lest thereby he should irritate his Spanish subjects. It was this capacity for large consideration that gave Charles V. his power in the future ; his motives were hard to discover, but they always rested on a view of his entire obligations, and were dictated by reasons known only to himself. Even Wolsey did not understand the Emperor's motives, which seemed to him entirely foolish. He allowed himself to take up a haughty position, which deeply offended Charles, who exclaimed angrily, "This cardinal will do everything his own way, and treats me as though I were a prisoner." Charles treasured up his resentment, of which Wolsey was entirely unconscious, and was determined not to allow so masterful a spirit to become more powerful.

He soon had an opportunity of acting on this deter-

mination, as the unexpected death of Pope Leo X. on
1st December naturally awakened hopes in Wolsey's
breast.   It was impossible that the foremost statesman
in Europe should not have had the legitimate aspiration
of reaching the highest office to which he could attain.
But though Wolsey was ready when the opportunity
came to press his own claims with vigour, it cannot be
said with fairness that his previous policy had been in
any way directed to that end, or that he had swerved
in the least from his own path to further his chances for
the papal office.   Indeed he had no reason for so doing,
as Leo was only forty-six years old when he died, and
his death was entirely unforeseen.   Moreover, we know
that when the Spanish envoys offered Wolsey the Emperor's help towards the Papacy in 1520, Wolsey refused
the offer; since then Charles at Bruges had repeated
the offer without being asked.   Now that a vacancy
had arisen, it was natural for Wolsey to attach some
weight to this promise, and Henry expressed himself
warmly in favour of Wolsey's election, and urged his
imperial ally to work by all means for that end.   He
sent to Rome his favourite secretary Pace to further it
by pressing representations to the cardinals.

It does not seem that Wolsey was very sanguine in
his expectations of being elected.   Leo X. had died at a
moment of great importance for Charles V.; in fact his
death had been brought about by the imprudence which
he showed in manifesting his delight at the success of the
imperial arms against Milan, and his prospect of the overthrow of France.   It was necessary for Charles that a Pope
should be elected who would hold to Leo's policy, and
would continue the alliance with England.   The man

who held in his hand the threads of Leo X.'s numerous
intrigues was his cousin, Cardinal Giulio de' Medici, and
Wolsey admitted the advantages to be gained by his
election. Wolsey at once declared that he submitted
his candidature to the decision of Henry VIII. and the
Emperor; if they thought that he was the best person to
promote their interests he would not shrink from the
labour; but he agreed that if his candidature were not
likely to be acceptable to the cardinals, the two monarchs
should unite in favour of Cardinal Medici. Charles's
ambassador wrote him that it would be well to act
carefully, as Wolsey was watching to see how much faith
he could put in the Emperor's protestations of goodwill.

So Charles was prepared, and acted with ambiguous
caution. He put off communicating with Henry as long
as he could; he regretted that he was in the Netherlands
instead of Germany, whence he could have made his
influence felt in Rome; he secretly ordered his ambassador in Rome to press for the election of Cardinal
Medici, but gave him no definite instructions about any
one else; finally he wrote a warm letter in favour of
Wolsey, which he either never sent at all, or sent too
late to be of any use, but which served as an enclosure
to satisfy Henry VIII. Wolsey was not deceived by
`this, and knew how papal elections might be influenced.
He told the Spanish ambassador that, if his master were
in earnest, he should order his troops to advance against
Rome, and should command the cardinals to elect his
nominee; he offered to provide 100,000 ducats to cover
the expenses of such action. When it came to the point
Wolsey was a very practical politician, and was under

no illusions about the .fair pretences of free choice which
surrounded a papal election. He treated it as a matter
to be settled by pressure from outside, according to the
will of the strongest. There is something revoltingly
cynical in this proposal. No doubt many men thought
like Wolsey, but no one else would have had the bold-
ness to speak out. Wolsey's outspokenness was of no
avail at the time, but it bore fruits afterwards. He
taught Henry VIII. to conceive the possibility of a short
way of dealing with refractory popes. He confirmed
his willing pupil in the belief that all things may be
achieved by the resolute will of one who rises above
prejudice and faces the world as it is. When he fell he
must have recognised that it was himself who trained the
arm which smote him.

In spite of Wolsey's advice Charles did not allow
Spanish influence to be unduly felt in the proceedings of
the conclave. Rarely had the cardinals been more undecided, and when they went into the conclave on
27th December, it was said that every one of them was
a candidate for the Papacy. The first point was to
exclude Cardinal Medici, and it could be plausibly urged
that it was dangerous to elect two successive popes from
the same family. Medici's opponents succeeded in
making his election impossible, but could not agree upon
a candidate of their own; while Medici tried to bring
about the election of some one who would be favourable
to the Emperor. At last in weariness the cardinals
turned their thoughts to some one who was not present.
Wolsey was proposed, and received seven votes; but
Medici was waiting his time, and put forward Cardinal Adrian of Utrecht, who had been Charles's tutor,

and was then governing Spain in his master's name.
Both parties agreed on him, chiefly because he was
personally unknown to any of the cardinals, had
given no offence, was well advanced in years, and was
reckoned to be of a quiet disposition, so that every one
had hopes of guiding his counsels. It was clear that the
imperialists were strongest in the conclave, and of all
the imperialist candidates Adrian was the least offensive
to the French. One thing is quite clear, that Charles V.
had not the least intention of helping Wolsey.

Wolsey probably knew this well enough, and was not
disappointed. He bore the Emperor no ill-will for his
lukewarmness; indeed he had no ground for expecting
anything else. Wolsey's aim was not the same as that
of Charles, and Charles had had sufficient opportunity
to discover the difference between them. Probably
Wolsey saw that the alliance between England and the
Emperor would not be of long duration, as there was no
real identity of interests. Henry VIII. was dazzled for
a moment with the prospect of asserting the English
claims on France; he was glad to find himself at one
with his queen, who was overjoyed at the prospect of a
family alliance with her own beloved land of Spain.
The English nobles rejoiced at an opportunity to display
their prowess, and hoped in time of war to recover the
influence and position of which they had been deprived
by an upstart priest. The sentiment of hostility to
France was still strong amongst the English people, and
the allurements of a spirited foreign policy were many.
But as a matter of fact England was ill prepared for
war; and though the people might throw up their caps
at first, they would not long consent to pay for a war

which brought them no profits. And the profits were not likely to be great, for Charles had no wish to see England's importance increased. He desired only English help to achieve his own purposes, and was no more trustworthy as an ally than had been his grandfather Ferdinand.

However, war had been agreed upon, and all that Wolsey could do was to try and put off its declaration until he had secured sufficient assurance that English money was not to be spent to no purpose. Charles V., who was in sore straits for money, asked for a loan from England, to which Wolsey answered that England could not declare war till the loan was repaid. He insisted that no declaration of war should be made till the Emperor had fulfilled his promise to pay a visit to England, a promise which Charles's want of money rendered him unable for some time to keep.

But however much Wolsey might try to put off the declaration of war, it was inevitable. Francis could not be expected, for all Wolsey's fine promises, to continue his payments for Tournai to so doubtful an ally as Henry, nor could he resist from crippling England as far as he could. The Duke of Albany went back to Scotland ; and in the beginning of May Francis ordered the seizure of goods lying at Bordeaux for shipment to England. This led to retaliation on the part of England, and war was declared against France on 28th May 1522.

This coincided with the visit of Charles V. to London, where he was magnificently entertained for a month, while the treaty of alliance was being finally brought into shape by Wolsey and Gattinara. Wolsey contented

himself with providing that the alliance did not go
further than had been agreed at Bruges, and that England's interests were secured by an undertaking from
Charles that he would pay the loss which Henry VIII.
sustained by the withdrawal of the French instalments
for Tournai. When the treaty was signed it was Wolsey
who, as papal legate, submitted both princes to ecclesiastical censures in case of a breach of its provisions.
Moreover, Charles granted Wolsey a pension of 9000
crowns in compensation for his loss from Tournai, and
renewed his empty promise of raising him to the
Papacy.

It was one thing to declare war and another to carry
it on with good effect. England, in spite of all the
delays which Wolsey had contrived to interpose, was
still unprepared. It was late in the autumn before
forces could be put in the field, and the troops of
Charles V. were too few for a joint undertaking of any
importance. The allies contented themselves with in-
vading Picardy, where they committed useless atrocities,
burning houses, devastating the country, and working
all the mischief that they could. They did not advance
into the centre of France, and no army met them in the
field ; in the middle of October they retired ingloriously.
It is hard to discover the purpose of such an expedition.
The damage done was not enough to weaken France
materially, and such a display of barbarity was ill suited
to win the French people to favour Henry VIII.'s claim
to be their rightful lord. If Francis I. had been un
popular before, he was now raised to the position of a
national leader whose help was necessary for the protection of his subjects.

The futile result of this expedition caused mutual recriminations between the new allies. The imperialists complained that the English had come too late; the English answered that they had not been properly supported. There were no signs of mutual confidence; and the two ministers, Wolsey and Gattinara, were avowed enemies, and did not conceal their hostility. The alliance with the Emperor did not show signs of prospering from the beginning.

The proceedings of the Earl of Surrey and the direction of the campaign were not Wolsey's concern. He was employed nearer home, in keeping a watchful eye on Scotland, which threatened to be a hindrance to Henry VIII.'s great undertakings abroad. The return of the Duke of Albany in December 1521 was a direct threat of war. Albany was nominally regent, but had found his office troublesome, and had preferred to spend the last five years in the gaieties of the French Court rather than among the rugged nobles of Scotland. They were years when France was at peace with England and had little interest in Scottish affairs; so Queen Margaret might quarrel with her husband at leisure, while the Scottish lords distributed themselves between the two parties as suited them best. But when war between France and England was approaching, the Duke of Albany was sent back by Francis I. to his post as agent for France in Scottish affairs. Queen Margaret welcomed him with joy, hoping that he would further her plan of gaining a divorce from the Earl of Angus. Before this union of forces the English party in Scotland was powerless. It was in vain that Henry VIII. tried by menaces to influence either his sister or the Scottish lords. As soon

as the English forces sailed for France Albany prepared
to invade England.

It was lucky for Henry VIII that he was well served
on the Borders by Lord Dacre of Naworth, who managed
to show the Scots the measure of Albany's incapacity.
Dacre began negotiations with Albany, to save time ; and
when, in September, the Scottish forces passed the
Border, Albany was willing to make a truce. As a
matter of fact, England was totally unprepared to repel
an invasion, and Albany might have dictated his own
terms. But Dacre, in Carlisle, which he could not defend, maintained his courage, and showed no signs of
fear. He managed to blind Albany to the real state of
affairs, and kept him from approaching to the crumbling
walls of Carlisle. He advanced to the Debatable Land
to meet him, and "with a high voice" demanded the
reason of his coming ; and the parley thus begun ended
in the conclusion of a month's truce. Wolsey was overjoyed at this result, but yet found it necessary to inter-
cede with the king for Dacre's pardon, as he had no
authority to make terms with the enemy ; and Dacre
was not only forgiven, but thanked. This futile end to
an expedition for which 80,000 soldiers had been raised
ruined Albany's influence, and he again retired to France
at the end of October.

Wolsey at once saw the risk which England had run.
A successful invasion on the part of the Scots would
have been a severe blow to England's military reputation ; and Wolsey determined to be secure on the
Scottish side for the future. The Earl of Surrey, on his
return from his expedition in France, was put in charge
of the defences of the Border, and everything was done

to humour Queen Margaret, and convince her that she had more to gain from the favour of her brother than from the help of the Duke of Albany. Moreover, Wolsey, already convinced of the uselessness of the war against France, was still ready to gain from it all that he could, and strove to use the threat of danger from Scotland as a means of withdrawing from war and gaining a signal triumph. Francis I., unable to defend himself, tried to separate his enemies, and turned to Charles V. with offers of a truce. When this was refused, he repeated his proposals to England, and Wolsey saw his opportunity. He represented to Charles that so long as England was menaced by Scotland she could send little effective help abroad; if Scotland were crushed she would be free again. He suggested that the Emperor had little to win by military enterprises undertaken with such slight preparation as the last campaign; would he not make truce for a year, not comprehending the realm of Scotland?

The suggestion was almost too palpable. Gattinara answered that Henry wished to use his forces for his private advantage, and neglected the common interest of the alliance. Again bitter complaints were made of Wolsey's lukewarmness Again the two allies jealously watched each other lest either should gain an advantage by making a separate alliance with France. And while they were thus engaged the common enemy of Christendom was advancing, and Rhodes fell before the Turkish arms. It was in vain that Adrian VI. lamented and wept; in vain he implored for succours. Fair promises alone were given him. Europe was too much intent on the duel between Francis and Charles to think

seriously of anything else.   The entreaties of the Pope
were only regarded by all parties as a good means of
enabling them to throw a decent veil over any measure
which their own interests might prompt.   They might
declare that it was taken for the sake of the holy war;
they might claim that they had acted from a desire to
fulfil the Pope's behest.

So things stood in the beginning of 1523, when an
unexpected event revived the military spirit of Henry
VIII., and brought the two half-hearted allies once more
closely together, by the prospect which it afforded of
striking a deadly blow at France.   The chief of the
nobles of France, the sole survivor of the great feudatories,
the Constable of Bourbon, was most unwisely affronted
by Francis I., at a time when he needed to rally all his
subjects round him.   Not only was Bourbon affronted,
but also a lawsuit was instituted against him, which
threatened to deprive him of the greater part of his
possessions.   Bourbon, who could bring into the field
6000 men, did not find his patriotism strong enough to
endure this wrong.   He opened up secret negotiations
with Charles, who disclosed the matter to Henry.
Henry's ambition was at once fired.   He saw Francis I.,
hopelessly weakened by a defection of the chief nobles,
incapable of withstanding an attack upon the interior of
his land, so that the English troops might conquer the
old provinces which England still claimed, and victory
might place upon his head the crown of France.

Wolsey was not misled by this fantastic prospect, but
as a campaign was imminent, took all the precautions
he could that it should be as little costly as possible to
England, and that Charles should bear his full share of

the expense. He demanded, moreover, that Bourbon
should acknowledge Henry VIII. as the rightful King of
France—a demand which was by no means acceptable to
Charles. He sent an envoy of his own to confer with
Bourbon, but his envoy was delayed on the way, so that
the agreement was framed in the imperial interests alone,
and the demands of Henry were little heeded. The
agreement was that Bourbon should receive the hand of
one of the Emperor's sisters, and should receive a subsidy
of 200,000 crowns to be paid equally by Henry and
Charles; the question of the recognition of Henry
as rightful King of France was to be left to the
decision of the Emperor.

The plan of the campaign was quickly settled.
Charles, with 20,000 men, was to advance into Guienne;
Henry, with 15,000 English, supported by 6000 Nether-
landers, was to advance through Picardy; 10,000
Germans were to advance through Burgundy; and
Bourbon was to head a body of dissatisfied nobles of
France. It was an excellent plan on paper; and, indeed,
the position of France seemed hopeless enough. Francis
I. had squandered his people's money, and was exceedingly unpopular; Wolsey's diplomacy had helped to win
over the Swiss to the imperial alliance; and the inde-
fatigable secretary Pace had been sent to Venice to
detach the republic from its connexion with France. It
was believed that Wolsey was jealous of Pace's influence
with Henry VIII., and contrived to keep him employed
on embassies which removed him from the Court. At
all events, he certainly kept him busily employed till his
health gave way under the excessive pressure. To lend
greater weight to Pace's arguments, Wolsey descended

to an act of overbearing insolence. Some Venetian
galleys trading with Flanders put in at Plymouth during
a storm ; they were laid under an embargo, and were
detained on many flimsy pretexts. It was in vain that
the Venetian ambassador remonstrated ; Wolsey always
had a plausible answer. Probably he wished to show
Venice that its trading interests required the friendship of England. At all events the galleys were not
released till Venice was on the point of joining the
imperial alliance. Even then Wolsey had the meanness
to carry off a couple of guns from each vessel, and Venice
had to make a present of them to the English king with
as much grace as the circumstances allowed. This little
incident certainly shows Wolsey's conduct at its worst,
and confirms the impression of contemporaries, that he
had to some degree the insolence of an upstart, and
sometimes overrode the weak in a way to leave behind
a bitter feeling of resentment.

However, Venice joined the Emperor, and Pope
Adrian VI., who had pursued hitherto a policy of
pacification, was at last overborne by the pressure of
England and the Emperor, so that he entered into a
defensive league against France. Thus France was
entirely isolated. Distrusted at home and unbefriended
abroad, she seemed to be a prey to her enemies ;
and Henry's hopes rose so high that he gleefully
looked forward to being recognised as " governor of
France," and that " they should by this means make a
way for him as King Richard did for his father."
Wiser men shook their heads at the king's infatuation
" I pray God," wrote More to Wolsey, " if it be good
for his Grace and for this realm that then it may prove

so; and else in the stead thereof I pray God send his grace an honourable and profitable peace."

The spirit that breathes through this prayer is not a martial spirit, and no doubt More's feelings represented those of Wolsey, who, though carried away by the king's military zeal, had little hopes of any great success, and such hopes as he had were rapidly destroyed. The campaign did not begin till the end of September; the contingent from the Netherlands was late in appearing and was ill supplied with food. Till the last moment Wolsey urged, as the first object of the campaign, the siege of Boulogne, which, if successful, would have given England a second stronghold on the French coast; but Wolsey was overruled, and an expedition into the interior of France was preferred. It was a repetition of the raid made in the last year, and was equally futile. The army advanced to Montdidier, and expected tidings of its confederate; but nothing was to be heard of Bourbon; his lanzknechts began to devastate France and then disbanded. The army of Charles V. contented itself with taking Fontarabia, and did not co-operate with the English forces After the capture of Montdidier the troops, who were attacked by sickness, and had difficulty in finding provisions, withdrew to the coast; and the Duke of Suffolk brought back his costly army without having obtained anything of service to England. This expedition, which was to do so much, was a total failure—there was positively nothing to be shown in return for all the money spent.

Again the wisdom of Wolsey's policy was fully justified. He was right in thinking that England had neither troops nor generals who were sufficient for an expedition on the Continent, where there was nothing tangible to be gained. So long as England was a neutral and mediating power she could pursue her own interests ; but her threats were more efficacious than her performances. She could not conquer unaided, and her allies had no intention of allowing her to win more than empty glory. Even this had been denied in the last campaigns. England had incurred debts which her people could ill afford to pay, and had only lowered her reputation by a display of military incompetence. Moreover, her expedition against France involved her in the usual difficulties on the side of Scotland. Again there was a devastating war along the Border ; again the Duke of Albany was sent from France and raised an army for the invasion of England. But this time Wolsey had taken his precautions, and the Earl of Surrey was ready to march against him. When in November Albany crossed the Tweed and besieged the Castle of Wark, Surrey took the field, and again Albany showed his incapacity as a leader. He retired before Surrey's advance, and wished to retire to France. but was prevented by the Scottish lords. Again the Border raids went on with their merciless slaughter and plunder, amidst which was developed the sternness and severity which still mark the character of the northern folk.

Still, though the Scots might be defeated in the field, their defeat and suffering only served to strengthen the spirit of national independence. The subjugation of Scotland to England was hindered, not helped, by the alliance with the Emperor, which only drew Scotland

nearer to France, and kept alive the old feeling of
hostility. It was hard to see what England had to gain
from the imperial alliance, and events soon proved that
Charles V. pursued his own interests without much
thought of the wishes of Henry VIII.

On 14th September died Pope Adrian VI., a weary
and disappointed man. Again there was a prospect of
Wolsey's election to the papacy; again it might be
seen how much Charles V. would do for his English
ally. Wolsey had little hope of his good offices, and
was his own negotiator in the matter. He was not
sanguine about his prospects of success, as he knew
that Cardinal Medici was powerful in Rome; and the
disasters of the pontificate of Adrian VI. led the
cardinals to wish for a return to the old policy of Leo
X., of which Medici held the threads. So two letters
were sent to the English representatives in Rome, one
in behalf of Wolsey, the other in behalf of Medici. If
things were going for Medici, Wolsey was not to be
pressed; only in case of a disagreement was Wolsey to
be put forward, and then no effort was to be spared;
money was to be of no object, as Henry would make
good any promises made on his behalf to secure Wolsey's
election.

The conclave was protracted; it sat from 1st October to 17th November, and there was ample opportunity for Charles to have made his influence felt in
Wolsey's behalf. He professed to Henry that he was
doing so. He wrote a letter recommending Wolsey to
his envoy in Rome, and then gave orders that the
courier who carried the letter should be detained on the
way. Really his influence was being used for Medici,

and though a strong party in the conclave opposed
Medici's election, it does not appear that Wolsey was
ever put forward as a competitor.   The cardinals would
hear nothing of a foreigner, and the stubbornness of
Medici's party was at length rewarded by his election.
There is no trace that Wolsey was keenly disappointed
at this result. In announcing it to Henry VIII., he wrote,
"For my part, as I take God to record, I am more
joyous thereof than if it had fortuned upon my person,
knowing his excellent qualities most meet for the same,
and how great and sure a friend your Grace and the
Emperor be like to have of him, and I so good a
father."

Few popes came to their office amid greater expectations, and few more entirely disappointed them than
did Guilio de' Medici.   Clement VII., whose election
Charles, Henry, and Wolsey united in greeting with
joy, suffered in a brief space entire humiliation at the
hands of Charles, caused the downfall of Wolsey, and
drove Henry to sever the bond between the English
Church and the Holy See.   It is impossible not to
think how different would have been the course of
events if Wolsey had presided over the destinies of the
Church

CHAPTER VII

RENEWAL OF PEACE

1523–1527

THE events of the year 1523 had practically made an end of the imperial alliance. Henry VIII. was not in a position to go to war again, and his confidence in Charles V.'s good intentions towards him was dispelled. Charles and Francis had had enough of war, and both of them secretly desired peace, but neither would make the first move towards it. Wolsey watched their movements keenly, and strove that English interests should not be entirely sacrificed in the pacification which seemed imminent. He strove to induce Charles to allow proposals of peace to proceed from England, which should arbitrate on the differences between him and Francis. He urged that in any negotiations which Charles himself undertook he was bound to consider how Henry could be recompensed for his losses. Moreover, he secretly opened up negotiations of his own with the French Court, and used the imperial alliance as a means to heighten England's value to France.

The more Wolsey watched events the more he became convinced that the best thing was to make a separate peace with France, yet in such a way as to avoid an open breach with the Emperor. There were other reasons besides the failure of military expeditions, and the distrust in any good result from their continuance, which impelled Wolsey to a pacific policy. He knew only too well that war was impossible, and that the country could not bear the continued drain on its resources. If Henry VII. had developed the royal power by a parsimony which enabled him to be free from parliamentary control, Henry VIII. had dazzled his people by the splendour of royalty, and had displayed his magnificence to such an extent that Englishmen were beginning to doubt if they could afford much longer to be so important, or rather if England's importance in Continental affairs were worth all the money that it cost. Of late years the weight of taxation had become oppressive, and the expenses of the last campaign were difficult to meet. .-

There was no difference between the national revenue and the royal revenue in Wolsey's days. The king took all the money he could get, and spent it as he thought good ; if he went to war he expected his people to pay for it. In an ordinary way the king was well provided for by his feudal dues and the proceeds of customs, tonnage and poundage, and the tax on wool, wool-fells, and leather. When extraordinary expenses were incurred Parliament was summoned, and granted taxes to the king. Their vote was reckoned on an old assessment of tenths and fifteenths of the value of chattels possessed by the baronage and the commons ; and when Parliament made this grant the clergy in their convocation granted a tenth of clerical incomes. The value of a tenth and fifteenth was £30,000 ; of a clerical tenth £10,000 ; so that the usual grant in case of an emergency amounted to £40,000 from the whole realm. For his expedition of 1513 Henry obtained a vote of two tenths and fifteenths, besides a subsidy of a graduated income and property tax which was estimated to produce £160,000, and this had to be supplemented by a further grant of tenths and fifteenths in 1515.

It was in 1515 that Wolsey became Chancellor, and with that office assumed the entire responsibility for all affairs of state. He managed to introduce some order into the finances, and during the years of pacific diplomacy things went tolerably well. But the French expeditions were costly, and in April 1523 Parliament had to be summoned to pay the king's debts. The war against France was popular, and men were willing to contribute.

So on 15th April Henry VIII. opened Parliament, and Tunstal, Bishop of London, delivered the usual oration in praise of the king and grief over the evils of the time. The Commons departed, and elected as their Speaker Sir Thomas More, who had already abandoned the quiet paths of literature for the stormy sea of politics. The king's assent was given in the usual manner to his appointment, and the session was adjourned. The Commons doubtless began to take financial matters under their consideration, but it was thought desirable that they should have a definite statement of the national needs. On 29th April Wolsey went to the House, and after urging the importance of the interests at stake in the war, proposed a subsidy of £800,000, to be raised according to an old method, by a tax of four shillings in the pound on all goods and lands. Next day there was much debate on this proposal; it was urged that the sudden withdrawal of so large an amount of ready money would seriously affect the currency, and was indeed almost impossible. A committee was appointed to represent to Wolsey that this was the sense of the House, and beg him to induce the king to moderate his demands. Wolsey answered that he would rather have his tongue pulled out with red-hot pincers than carry such a message to the king.

The Commons in a melancholy mood renewed their debate till Wolsey entered the House and desired to reason with those who opposed his demands. On this Sir Thomas More, as Speaker, defended the privilege of the House by saying, "That it was the order of that House to hear and not to reason save among themselves." Whereupon Wolsey was obliged to content himself with answering such objections as had come to his ear. He argued, it would seem with vigour, that the country was much richer than they thought, and he told them some unpleasant truths, which came with ill grace from himself, about the prevalence of luxury. After his departure the debate continued till the House agreed to grant two shillings in the pound on all incomes of £20 a year and upwards; one shilling on all between £20 and £2; and fourpence on all incomes under £2; this payment to be extended over two years. This was increased by a county member, who said, "Let us gentlemen of £50 a year and upwards give the king of our lands a shilling in the pound, to be paid in two years." The borough members stood aloof, and allowed the landholders to tax themselves an extra shilling in the pound if they chose to do so. This was voted on 21st May, and Parliament was prorogued till 10th June. Meanwhile popular feeling was greatly moved by rumours of an unprecedented tax, and what was really done was grossly exaggerated on all sides. As the members left the House an angry crowd greeted them with jeers. "We hear say that you will grant four shillings in the pound. Do so, and go home, we advise you." Really the members had done the best they could, and worse things were in store for them. For when the session was resumed the knights of the shire showed some resentment that they had been allowed to outdo the burgesses in liberality. They proposed that as they had agreed to pay a shilling in the pound on land assessed over £50 in the third year, so a like payment should be made in the fourth year on all goods over the value of £50. There was a stormy debate on this motion; but Sir Thomas More at length made peace, and it was passed. Thus Wolsey, on the whole, had contrived to obtain something resembling his original proposal, but the payments were spread over a period of four years. After this Wolsey, at the prorogation of Parliament, could afford to thank the Commons on the king's behalf, and assure them that "his Grace would in such wise employ their loving contribution as should be for the defence of his realm and of his subjects, and the persecution and pressing of his enemy."

Yet, however Wolsey might rejoice in his success, he knew that he had received a serious warning, which he was bound to lay to heart. He had been faithful to the king, and had done his best to carry out his views.

The war with France was none of his advising, and he had no hopes of any advantage from it ; yet he was willing to take all the blame of measures which inwardly he disapproved. He stood forward and assumed the unpopularity of taxation, whose necessity he deplored. Henry spent the nation's money at his pleasure, and Wolsey undertook the ungrateful task of squeezing supplies from a reluctant Parliament, while the king sat a benevolent spectator in the background. Henry took all the glory, and left Wolsey to do all the unpleasant work. Wolsey stood between the national temper and the king; he felt that he could not stand under the odium of accomplishing many more such reconciliations. England had reached the limit of its aspirations after national glory. For the future Wolsey must maintain the king's honour without appealing to the national pocket.

There was no prospect of obtaining further supplies from Parliament, and the best way to pay the expenses of a futile war was by making a lucrative peace. Wolsey tried to induce Francis I. to renew his financial agreement with Henry VIII. which the war had broken off ; and to bring pressure to bear upon him for this purpose, was willing to continue with Charles V. negotiations for a fresh undertaking.

So in June the unwearied Pace was sent to Bourbon's camp to promise England's help on terms which Wolsey knew were sure to be refused. England would again join in a campaign against France in the north, provided Bourbon, by an invasion of Provence, succeeded in raising a rebellion against Francis I., and would take an oath of allegiance to the English king as lord of France. Bour-

bon sorely needed money, and did all he could to win over
Pace. He secretly took an oath of fidelity, not of allegiance; and Pace was impressed with admiration of his genius
and believed in his chances of success. Wolsey was
coldly cautious towards Pace's enthusiasm, and the result
was a breach between them. Pace openly blamed Wolsey,
as Wingfield had done before, and pressed for money
and an armed demonstration. Wolsey soberly rebuked
his lack of judgment by setting before him a well-considered survey of the political chances. His caution proved
to be justified, as Bourbon's invasion of Provence was a
failure. Wolsey gained all that he needed by his pre-
tence of helping Bourbon; he induced the French
Court to undertake negotiations seriously by means of
secret envoys who were sent to London.

Still Wolsey did not hide from himself the difficulties in the way of an alliance with France which
would satisfy Henry VIII. or bring substantial advantage to the country. However, on one point he managed
to obtain an immediate advantage. He always kept
his eye on Scotland, and now used the first signs of returning friendliness on the part of France to further
his scheme of restoring English influence in that
country. In June the Duke of Albany was recalled to
France, and Wolsey set to work to win back Queen
Margaret to her brother's cause. He seems to have
despaired of blandishments, and contrived a way to
have a more powerful weapon. Margaret's husband,
the Earl of Angus, had been sent by Albany to France,
where he was carefully guarded. On the first signs
of renewed friendliness between England and France a
hint from Wolsey procured him an opportunity of

escaping to England.   With Angus at his disposal
Wolsey urged Maigaret to be reconciled to her
husband, and terrified her by the prospect of alternately
restoring him to Scotland.   By playing cleverly on her
personal feelings, Wolsey led her by degrees to accept
his own plan for freeing Scotland from Albany and
French interference.   He urged that the young king was
now old enough to rule for himself, and promised Margaret help to secure her supremacy in his council.   At
the same time he won over the Scottish lords by the
prospect of a marriage between James and Mary of England, who was still Henry VIII.'s heir.   In August
James V. was set up as king, and the Scottish Parliament approved of the English marriage.   Again Wolsey
won a signal triumph, and accomplished by diplomacy
what the sword had been unable to achieve.

We need not follow the complicated diplomacy of the
year 1524, which was transferred to Italy, whither Francis
I. had pursued Bourbon and was engaged in the siege
of Pavia.   It is enough to say that Wolsey pursued a
cautious course : if Francis won the day in Italy he was
ready to treat with him liberally : if the imperial arms
prevailed, then he could sell England's alliance more
dearly.   But this cautious attitude was displeasing
to Charles, whose ambassador in London, De Praet,
complained without ceasing of the growing coldness of
Henry and Wolsey.   Wolsey kept a sharp watch on
De Praet, and resented his keen-sightedness ; finally,
in February 1525, De Praet's despatches were inter-
cepted, and he was called before the Council, when
Wolsey charged him with untruth.   De Praet answered
by complaining that his privileges as an ambassador had

been violated. He was ordered to confine himself to his own house till the king had written to the Emperor about his conduct.

This was indeed an unheard-of treatment for the ambassador of an ally, and we can scarcely attribute it merely to personal spite on the part of so skilled a statesman as Wolsey. Perhaps it was a deliberate plan to cause a personal breach between Henry and the Emperor. No doubt Henry's own feelings were towards Charles rather than Francis, and it seems probable that Wolsey wished to show his master that Charles was only trying to make use of his friendship for his own purposes. The despatches of Charles's envoy were opened and their contents made known to Henry for some time before Wolsey took any open action. He acted when he saw his master sufficiently irritated, and he probably suggested that the best way to give Charles a lesson was by an attack upon his ambassador. This proposal agreed with the high-handed manner of action which Henry loved to adopt. It gave him a chance of asserting his own conception of his dignity, and he challenged Charles to say if he identified himself with his ambassador's sentiments.

Under any circumstances it was an audacious step, and as things turned out it was an unfortunate one. Within a few days the news reached England that Francis had been attacked at Pavia by the imperial forces, had been entirely routed, and was a prisoner in the hands of Charles. Though Wolsey was prepared for some success of the imperial arms, he was taken aback at the decisiveness of the stroke. His time for widening the breach between Charles and Henry had not been well chosen.

However, Charles saw that he could not pursue his
victory without money, and to obtain money he must
adopt an appearance of moderation. So he professed in
Italy willingness to forget the past, and he avoided a
quarrel with England He treated the insult to his
ambassador as the result of a personal misunder-
standing. Henry complained of De Praet's unfriendly
bearing; Charles assured him that no offence was
intended. Both parties saved their dignity; De Praet
was recalled, and another ambassador was sent in his
stead. Wolsey saw that he had been precipitate, and
hastened to withdraw his false step ; Henry lent
him his countenance, but can scarcely have relished
doing so. Wolsey knew that his difficulties were increased. The victory of Charles again drew Henry to
his side and revived his projects of conquest at the
expense of France, now left helpless by its king's captivity. As the defection of Bourbon had formerly
awakened Henry's hopes, so now did the captivity
of Francis. Again Wolsey's pacific plans were shattered ;
again he was driven to undertake the preparations for a
war of which his judgment disapproved.

Indeed Wolsey knew that war was absolutely impossible for want of money ; but it was useless to say so to
the king. He was bound to try and raise supplies by
some means or other, and his experience of the last Parliament had shown him that there was no more to be
obtained from that source. In his extremity Wolsey
undertook the responsibility of reviving a feudal obliga-
tion which had long been forgotten. He announced
that the king purposed to pass the sea in person, and
demanded that the goodwill of his subjects should provide

for his proper equipment. But the goodwill of the
people was not allowed the privilege of spontaneous
generosity. Commissioners were appointed in every
shire to assess men's property, and require a sixth part of
it for the king's needs. Wolsey himself addressed the
citizens of London. When they gave a feeble assent to
his request for advice, " whether they thought it convenient that the king should pass the sea with an army
or not," he proceeded, " Then he must go like a prince,
which cannot be without your aid." He unfolded his proposals for a grant of 3s. 4d. in the pound on £50 and
upwards, 2s. 8d. on £20 and upwards, and 1s. in the pound
on £1 and upwards. Some one pleaded that the times
were bad. " Sirs," said Wolsey, "speak not to break what
is concluded, for some shall not pay even a tenth ; and it
were better that a few should suffer indigence than the
king at this time should lack. Beware, therefore, and
resist not, nor ruffle not in this case ; otherwise it may
fortune to cost some their heads." This was indeed a
high-handed way of dealing with a public meeting,
which was only summoned to hear the full measure of
the coming calamity. We cannot wonder that "all
people cursed the cardinal and his adherents as subver-
ters of the laws and liberty of England." Nor was
Wolsey ignorant of the unpopularity which he incurred ,
but there was no escape possible. He rested only on the
king's favour, and he knew that the king's personal affection for him had grown colder. He was no longer the
king's friend and tutor, inspiring him with his own lofty
ideas and slowly revealing his far-reaching schemes.
Late years had seen Wolsey immersed in the business of
the State, while the king pursued his own pleasures, sur-

rounded by companions who did their utmost to undermine Wolsey's influence. They advocated war, while he
longed for peace; they encouraged the royal extravagance, while he worked for economy; they favoured the
imperial alliance and humoured Henry's dreams of the
conquest of France, while Wolsey saw that England's
strength lay in a powerful neutrality. The king's plans
had deviated from the lines which Wolsey had designed,
and the king's arbitrary temper had grown more
impatient of restraint. Wolsey had imperceptibly
slipped from the position of a friend to that of a servant,
and he was dimly conscious that his continuance in the
royal service depended on his continued usefulness.
Whatever the king required he was bound to provide.

So Wolsey strained every nerve to fill the royal
coffers by the device of an "Amicable Loan," which raised
a storm of popular indignation. Men said with truth
that they had not yet paid the subsidy voted by Parliament, and already they were exposed to a new exac-
tion. Coin had never been plentiful in England, and at
that time it was exceptionally scarce. The commissioners
in the different shires all reported the exceeding difficulty
which they met with in the discharge of their unpleasant
duty. It soon became clear to Wolsey that his demand
had overshot the limits of prudence, and that money
could not be raised on the basis of the parliamentary
assessment without the risk of a rebellion. Accordingly
Wolsey withdrew from his original proposal. He sent
for the mayor and corporation of London and told them,
in the fictitious language in which constitutional procedure is always veiled, "I kneeled down to his Grace,
showing him both your good minds towards him and also

the charge you continually sustain, the which, at my
desire and petition, was content to call in and abrogate
the same commission." The attempt to raise money on
the basis of each man's ratable value was abandoned,
and the more usual method of a benevolence was substituted in its stead.

This, however, was not much more acceptable.
Again Wolsey summoned the mayor and corporation;
but they had now grown bolder, and pleaded that bene-
volences had been abolished by the statute of Richard III.
Wolsey angrily answered that Richard was a usurper
and a murderer of his nephews; how could his acts
be good? " An it please your Grace," was the answer,
"although he did evil, yet in his time were many good
acts made not by him only, but by the consent of the
body of the whole realm, which is Parliament." There
was nothing more to be said, and Wolsey had to content himself with leaving every man to contribute
privily what he would. It did not seem that this spontaneous liberality went far to replenish the royal
exchequer.

What happened in London was repeated in different
forms in various parts of England. In Norwich there
was a tumult, which it needed the presence of the Duke
of Norfolk to appease. He asked the confused assembly
who was their captain, and bade that he should speak.
Then out spake one John Greene, a man of fifty years.
"My lord, since you ask who is our captain, forsooth,
his name is Poverty; for he and his cousin Necessity
have brought us to this doing. For all these persons
and many more live not of ourselves, but we live by the
substantial occupiers of this country; and yet they give

us so little wages for our workmanship that scarcely we
be able to live ; and thus in penury we pass the time,
we, our wives and children : and if they, by whom we
live, be brought in that case that they of their little cannot help us to earn our living, then must we perish and
die miserably.   I speak this, my lord : the clothmakers
have put away all their people, and a far greater number,
from work.   The husbandmen have put away their servants and given up household ; they say the king asketh
so much that they be not able to do as they have done
before this time, and then of necessity must we die
wretchedly."

John Greene's speech expressed only too truly the
condition of affairs in a period of social change.   The
old nobility had declined, and the old form of life
founded on feudalism was slowly passing away.   Trade was
becoming more important than agriculture ; the growth
of wool was more profitable than the growth of corn.   It
is true that England as a whole was growing richer, and
that the standard of comfort was rising ; but there was
a great displacement of labour, and consequent discontent.   The towns had thriven at the expense of the
country ; and in late years the war with France had
hindered trade with the Netherlands.   The custom
duties had diminished, the drain of bullion for war
expenses had crippled English commerce.   There had
been a succession of bad seasons, and every one had
begun to diminish his establishment and look more carefully after his expenditure.

All this was well known to the Duke of Norfolk, and
was laid before the king.   The commissions were recalled,
pardons were granted to the rioters, and the loan was

allowed to drop.   But Wolsey had to bear all the odium
of the unsuccessful attempt, while the king gained all the
popularity of abandoning it.   Yet Henry VIII. resented
the failure, and was angry with Wolsey for exposing him
to a rebuff.   In spite of his efforts Wolsey was ceasing
to be so useful as he had been before, and Henry began
to criticise his minister.   Brave and resolute as Wolsey
was, his labours and disappointments began to tell upon
him.   Since the failure of the Conference of Calais he
had been working not at the development of a policy
which he approved, but at the uncongenial task of
diminishing the dangers of a policy which he disapproved.   The effects of this constant anxiety told upon
his health and spirits, and still more upon his temper.
He might be as able and as firm as ever, but he no
longer had the same confidence in himself.

It was perhaps this feeling which led Wolsey to show
the king the extremity of his desire to serve him by
undertaking the desperate endeavour to wring more
money from an exhausted people.   Wolsey had done his
utmost to satisfy the king; he had accepted without a
murmur the burden of popular hatred which the attempt
was sure to bring.   There is a pathos in his words,
reported by an unfriendly hand, addressed to the
council: "Because every man layeth the burden from
him, I am content to take it on me, and to endure the
fume and noise of the people, for my goodwill towards
the king, and comfort of you, my lords and other the
king's councillors; but the eternal God knoweth all."
Nor was it enough that he submitted to the storm; he
wished to give the king a further proof of his devotion.
Though others might withhold their substance, yet he

would not. He offered the king his house at Hampton
Court, which he had built as his favourite retreat,
and had adorned to suit his taste. It was indeed a royal
gift, and Henry had no scruple in accepting it. But the
offer seems to show an uneasy desire to draw closer a
bond which had been gradually loosened, and renew an
intimacy which was perceptibly diminishing.

However, in one way Wolsey had a right to feel
satisfaction even in his ill-success. If money was not
to be had, war was impossible, and Wolsey might now
pursue his own policy and work for peace. He had to
face the actual facts that England was allied to Charles,
who had won a signal victory over Francis, and had
in his hands a mighty hostage in the person of the
King of France. His first object was to discover Charles
V.'s intentions, and prevent him from using his advantage solely for his own profit. Bishop Tunstal and Sir
Richard Wingfield were sent to Charles with orders
to put on a bold face, and find whether Charles thought
of dethroning Francis or releasing him for a ransom. In
the first case, they were to offer military aid from
England; in the second, they were to claim for England
a large share in the concessions to be wrung out of
Francis. The English demands were so exorbitant
that though they may have satisfied the fantastic aspirations of Henry, Wolsey must have known them to
be impossible. Under cover of a friendly proposal to
Charles he was really preparing the way for a breach.

Charles on his side was engaged in playing a similar
game. In spite of his success at Pavia he was really
helpless. He had no money, and the captivity of the
French king awakened so much alarm in Europe that

he felt compelled to use his advantage moderately.   As
a first measure he needed money, and saw no chance of
obtaining it save by marrying Isabella of Portùgal, who
would bring him a dowry of 1,000,000 golden crowns. For
this purpose he must free himself from the engagement
of the treaty of Windsor, by which he was betrothed to
Mary of England.   So he acted as Wolsey was acting
He professed a great desire to carry out his engagement
as a means of getting rid of it, and sent ambassadors to
ask that Mary and her dowry should be given up to him,
with a further loan of 200,000 ducats.

The two embassies had crossed on the way, and
Henry received Charles's communication as an answer
to his demands.   In this way it served Wolsey's
purpose admirably, for it showed clearly enough that the
interests of Henry and Charles were not the same.
Charles was bent upon pursuing his own advantage, and
was still willing to use Henry as a useful ally ; but
Henry saw nothing to be gained from the alliance, and
the time had come when some tangible gain was to be
secured from all his expenditure.   Hitherto he had been
personally on Charles's side, but in his conferences with
the imperial envoys in the month of June he made it
clear that his patience was exhausted.   Henceforth he
accepted Wolsey's views of peace with France.   If
Charles was striving to make what he could out of the
captivity of the French king, then England might as
well join in the scramble.   The misfortune of France
was England's opportunity.   If Charles was not willing
to share his gains with Henry, then Henry must pick up
what he could for himself.   It was an unwelcome conclusion for Charles, who hoped to bring the pressure of

irresistible necessity to bear on his captive. If England also joined in the bidding its competition would run down his price.

Moreover, this resolution of Henry made a great change in his domestic relations.   Queen Katharine was devoted to her nephew's interests, and had exercised considerable influence over her husband.   They talked together about politics, and Henry liked to move amidst acquiescent admiration.   All that was now at an end, as Katharine could not change her sympathies, and had not the tact to disguise her disapprobation.   From this time forward Henry did not treat her with the affection and familiarity which had been his wont, and when he made up his mind he did not scruple to emphasise his decision by his acts.   He had not been a faithful husband, but hitherto his infidelity had not been a cause of domestic discord.   He had an illegitimate son, Henry Fitzroy, by Elizabeth Blunt, one of the Queen's ladies-in-waiting ; and on 15th June he created this boy of six years old Duke of Richmond.   This he did with a display of pomp and ceremony which must have been very offensive to the Queen ; nor was the offence diminished when, a month afterwards, the boy was created Lord High Admiral of England.   Such an act was, to say the least, a taunt to Katharine that she had borne no son ; it was a public proclamation of the king's disappointment and discontent with his matrimonial lot. The luckless Katharine could make no complaint, and was forced to submit to the king's will ; but we cannot doubt that she put down to Wolsey what was not his due, and that Wolsey had to bear the hatred of her friends for the king's change of policy, and all that flowed from it

However, Wolsey's course was now clearly to dissolve
the imperial alliance without causing a breach.   For this
purpose he used Charles's desire for his Portuguese
marriage.   He offered to release Charles from his
engagement to Mary on condition that the treaty was
annulled, that he paid his debts to Henry, and concluded
a peace with France to England's satisfaction.   Charles
refused to take any step so decided, and the negotiations
proceeded.   But Wolsey's attention was not so much
directed to Charles as to France, where Louise, the king's
mother, was desperately striving to procure her son's
release.   In their dealings with France there was a
keen rivalry between England and the Emperor, which
should succeed in making terms soonest.   In this competition Wolsey had one advantage; he had already
learned the stubbornness of the national spirit of France,
and its willingness to submit to anything rather than
territorial loss.   So, while Charles haggled for provinces,
Wolsey demanded money.   He told the French envoys
that in order to make peace, without having won laurels
to justify it, Henry could not take less than 2,000,000
crowns, and he would hear of no abatement.   There
was much discussion of all the old claims of England for
compensation from France, but Wolsey knew the necessity of the moment, and carried all his points.

When the terms were agreed upon there was another
discussion about the security to be given.   Francis was
a prisoner in Spain, and though his mother was regent, a
doubt might be thrown upon her capacity to ratify such
an important treaty.   Wolsey would admit no doubts
in the matter.   He knew that peace with France would
not be popular, but he was determined that his master

should see its advantage in the substantial form of ready
money with good security for its payment. Besides
ratification by the regent he demanded the personal
security of several French nobles, of towns and local
estates. At length he was satisfied. The treaty was
signed on 30th August, and was published on 6th September. Henry was to receive 2,000,000 crowns in
annual instalments of 50,000; the treaty included
Scotland as an ally of France, and it was stipulated that
the Duke of Albany was not to return. Scotland, left
unprotected, was bound to follow France, and in January
1526 peace was signed with Scotland to the satisfaction
of both countries.

Wolsey could congratulate himself on the result of
his work. Again he had won for England a strong
position, by setting her in the forefront of the opposition
to the overweening power of the empire. Again had
England's action done much to restore the equilibrium
of Europe. This had been achieved solely by Wolsey's
diplomacy. Charles V. had received a blow which he
could neither parry nor resent. The French treaty
with England deprived Charles of the means of exercis-
ing irresistible pressure upon Francis, and encouraged
the Italian States to form an alliance against the Emperor.
Francis, weary of his long captivity, signed the treaty
of Madrid, and obtained his freedom in February 1526.
But he previously protested against it as extorted by
violence, and refused to surrender an inch of French
territory notwithstanding his promises. Charles gained
little by his victory at Pavia. His hands were again
full, as the Turks invaded Hungary, and Francis
joined the Italian League against him. He still had

every motive to keep on good terms with England, and Wolsey had no desire to precipitate a breach.

So Wolsey's policy for the future was one of caution and reserve. The king withdrew more and more from public affairs, and spent his time in hunting. His relations with Katharine became day by day more irksome, and he tried to forget his domestic life by leading a life of pleasure. Wolsey strove to hold the balance between Charles and Francis without unduly inclining to either side. Both wished to be on good terms with England, for neither was free from anxiety. The sons of Francis were hostages in Spain, and Charles was hampered by the opposition of the Italian League. Of this League Henry VIII. was a member, but he declined to give it any active support. The Italians, as usual, were divided, and Clement VII. was not the man to direct their distracted councils successfully. In September 1526 a small force of Spaniards, aided by a party amongst the Roman barons, surprised Rome, sacked the papal palace, and filled Clement with terror. Charles V. disavowed any share in this attack, and excused himself before Henry's remonstrances. But as Clement did not entirely amend his ways, the experiment was repeated on a larger scale. In May 1527 the imperial troops under the Duke of Bourbon and the German general George Frundsberg captured and plundered Rome, and took the Pope prisoner. This unwonted deed filled Europe with horror. It seemed as if the Emperor had joined the enemies of the Church.

During this period Wolsey had been cautiously drawing nearer to France. At first he only contemplated strengthening the ties which bound the two countries

together; but in the beginning of 1527 he was willing
to form a close alliance with France, which must lead to
a breach with the Emperor. French commissioners
came to London, and a proposal was made that Francis
should marry Mary, then a child of ten, though he was
betrothed to the Emperor's sister Eleanor. Wolsey's
demands were high : a perpetual peace between the two
countries, a perpetual pension of 50,000 crowns to the
English king, a tribute of salt, and the surrender of
Boulogne and Ardres. In the course of the discussion
the son of Francis, the Duke of Orleans, was substituted
for the father as Mary's husband ; on all other points
Wolsey had his will, and never did he show himself a
more consummate master of diplomacy. The treaty
was signed on 30th April. The debts of Charles were
transferred to Francis, and Wolsey could show that he
had made a substantial gain.

Doubtless Wolsey intended that this peace with
France should form the basis of a universal peace, which
he never ceased to pursue. The success of Charles V.
in Italy, and subsequent events at home, rapidly dispelled
his hopes Already the selfwill of Henry VIII. had
driven him to consent to measures which were against
his judgment ; the same selfwill, turned to domestic
and personal affairs, was already threatening to involve
Wolsey in a matter whose far-reaching effects no man
could foresee.

CHAPTER VIII

WE have been following the laborious career of Wolsey
in his direction of foreign affairs. He held in his hands
the threads of complicated negotiations, by which he
was endeavouring to assure England's power on the
Continent, not by means of war but by skilful diplomacy. In doing this he had to guard the commercial
relations of England with the Nethèrlands, and had also
to bow before the selfwill of the king, who insisted
on pursuing fantastic designs of personal aggrandisement. Still he steered a careful course amidst many
difficulties, though when he looked back upon his
labours of thirteen years he must have owned to serious
disappointment. Perhaps he sometimes asked himself
the question, if foreign policy was worthy of the best
attention of an English minister, if he had not erred in
adventuring on such large schemes abroad. There was
much to do at home ; many useful measures of reform
awaited only a convenient season. He had hoped, when
first he began his course, to have seen England long
before this time peaceful and powerful, the arbiter of
European affairs, a pattern to other kingdoms, dealing

honestly and sagaciously with the pressing needs of the time. He had laboured incessantly for that end, but it was as far off as ever. The year 1527 saw England exhausted by useless wars, and Europe plunged in irreconcilable strife. Wolsey's dream of a united Europe, cautiously moved by England's moderating counsels, had vanished before forces which he could not control.

Meanwhile domestic reforms had been thrust into the background. Wolsey was keenly alive to their importance, and had a distinct policy which he wished to carry out. He had carefully gathered into his hands the power which would enable him to act, but he could not find the time for definite action. Something he contrived to do, so as to prepare the way for more; but his schemes were never revealed in their entirety, though he trained the men who afterwards carried them out, though in a crude and brutal shape.

England was passing through a period of social change which necessitated a re-adjustment of old institutions. The decay of feudalism in the Wars of the Roses had been little noticed, but its results had been profound. In the sphere of government the check exercised by the barons on the Crown was destroyed. Henry VII. carefully depressed the baronage and spared the pockets of the people, who were willing to have the conduct of affairs in the hands of the king so long as he kept order and guarded the commercial interests, which were more and more absorbing national energies. The nation wished for a strong government to put down anarchy and maintain order; but the nation was not willing to bear the cost of a strong government on constitutional principles. Henry VII. soon found that he might do what

he liked provided he did not ask for money; he might
raise supplies by unconstitutional exactions on individuals
provided he did not embarrass the bulk of the middle
classes, who were busied with trade. The nobles, the
rich landowners, the wealthy merchants, were left to the
king's mercies; so long as the pockets of the commons
were spared they troubled themselves no further.

Henry VII. recognised this condition of national
feeling, and pursued a policy of levelling class privileges
and cautiously heeding the popular interests; by these
means he established the royal power on a strong basis,
and carried on his government through capable officials,
who took their instructions from himself. Some of the
old nobles held office, but they gradually were reduced
to the same level as the other officials with whom they
consorted. The power of the old nobility passed silently
away.

With this political change a social change corresponded
The barons of former years were great in proportion to
the number of their retainers and the strength of their
castles. Now retainers were put down by the Star
Chamber; and the feudal lord was turned into the
country gentleman. Land changed hands rapidly;
opulent merchants possessed themselves of estates. The
face of the country began to wear a new look, for the
new landlords did not desire a numerous tenantry but a
large income. The great trade of England was wool,
which was exported to Flanders. Tillage lands were
thrown into pasture; small holders found it more
difficult to live on their holdings; complaints were
heard that the country was being depopulated. England
was slowly passing through an economic change which

involved a displacement of population, and consequent misery on the labouring classes. No doubt there was a great increase in national prosperity; but prosperity was not universally diffused at once, and men were keenly conscious of present difficulties. Beneath the surface of society there was a widespread feeling of discontent.

Moreover, amongst thinking men a new spirit was beginning to prevail. In Italy this new spirit was manifest by quickened curiosity about the world and life, and found its expression in a study of classical antiquity. Curiosity soon led to criticism; and before the new criticism the old ideas on which the intellectual life of the Middle Ages was built were slowly passing away. Rhetoric took the place of logic, and the study of the classics superseded the study of theology. This movement of thought slowly found its way to England, where it began to influence the higher minds.

Thus England was going through a crisis politically, socially, and intellectually, when Wolsey undertook the management of affairs. This crisis was not acute, and did not call for immediate measures of direction; but Wolsey was aware of its existence, and had his own plans for the future. We must regret that he put foreign policy in the first place, and reserved his constructive measures for domestic affairs. The time seemed ripe for great achievements abroad, and Wolsey was hopeful of success. He may be pardoned for his lofty aspirations, for if he had succeeded England would have led the way in a deliberate settlement of many questions which concerned the wellbeing of the whole of Christendom. But success eluded Wolsey's grasp, and he fell from power before he had time to trace decidedly the

lines on which England might settle her problems for
herself; and when the solution came it was strangely
entangled in the personal questions which led to Wolsey's
fall from power. Yet even here we may doubt if the
measures of the English Reformation would have been
possible if Wolsey's mind had not inspired the king and
the nation with a heightened consciousness of England's
power and dignity. Wolsey's diplomacy at least tore
away all illusions about Pope and Emperor, and the
opinion of Europe, and taught Henry VIII. the measure
of his own strength.

It was impossible that Wolsey's powerful hand should
not leave its impression upon everything which it touched.
If Henry VIII. inherited a strong monarchy, Wolsey
made the basis of monarchical power still stronger. It
was natural that he should do so, as he owed his own
position entirely to the royal favour. But never had
any king so devoted a servant as had Henry VIII., in
Wolsey; and this devotion was not entirely due to
motives of selfish calculation or to personal attraction.
Wolsey saw in the royal power the only possible means
of holding England together and guiding it through the
dangers of impending change. In his eyes the king
and the king alone could collect and give expression to
the national will. England itself was unconscious of its
capacities, and was heedless about the future. The
nobles, so far as they had any policy, were only desirous
to win back their old position. The Church was no
longer the inspirer of popular aspirations or the bulwark
of popular freedom. Its riches were regarded with a
jealous eye by the middle classes, who were busied with
trade; the defects of its organisation had been deplored

by its most spiritually-minded sons for a century; its practices, if not its tenets, awakened the ridicule of men of intelligence; its revenues supplied the king with officials more than they supplied the country with faithful pastors; its leaders were content to look to the king for patronage and protection. The traders of the towns and the new landlords of the country appreciated the growth of their fortunes in a period of internal quiet, and dreaded anything that might bring back discord. The labouring classes felt that redress of their grievances was more possible from a far-off king than from landlords who, in their eyes, were bent upon extortion. Every class looked to the king, and was confident in his good intentions. We cannot wonder that Wolsey saw in the royal power the only possible instrument strong enough to work reforms, and set himself with goodwill to make that instrument efficacious.

So Wolsey was in no sense a constitutional minister, nor did he pay much heed to constitutional forms. Parliament was only summoned once during the time that he was in office, and then he tried to browbeat Parliament and set aside its privileges. In his view the only function of Parliament was to grant money for the king's needs. The king should say how much he needed, and Parliament ought only to advise how this sum might most conveniently be raised. We have seen that Wolsey failed in his attempt to convert Parliament into a submissive instrument of royal despotism. He under-estimated the strength of constitutional forms and the influence of precedent. Parliament was willing to do its utmost to meet the wishes of the king, but it would not submit to Wolsey's high-handed dictation. The

habits of diplomacy had impaired Wolsey's sagacity in
other fields ; he had been so busy in managing emperors
and kings that he had forgotten how to deal with his
fellow-countrymen. He was unwise in his attempt to
force the king's will upon Parliament as an unchangeable
law of its action. Henry VIII. looked on and learned
from Wolsey's failure, and when he took the management of Parliament into his own hands he showed himself a consummate master of that craft. His skill in this
direction has scarcely been sufficiently estimated, and
his success has been put down to the servility of Parliament. But Parliament was by no means servile under
Wolsey's overbearing treatment. If it was subservient
to Henry the reason is to be found in his excellent
tactics. He conciliated different interests at different
times ; he mixed the redress of acknowledged grievances
with the assertion of far-reaching claims ; he decked out
selfish motives in fair-sounding language ; he led men on
step by step till they were insensibly pledged to measures more drastic than they approved ; he kept the
threads of his policy in his own hands till the only
escape from utter confusion was an implicit confidence in
his wisdom ; he made it almost impossible for those who
were dissatisfied to find a point on which they could
establish a principle for resistance. He was so skilful that
Parliament at last gave him even the power over the
purse, and Henry, without raising a murmur, imposed taxes which Wolsey would not have dared to
suggest. It is impossible not to feel that Henry, perhaps
taught in some degree by Cromwell, understood the
temper of the English people far better than Wolsey
ever did. He established the royal power on a broader

K

and securer basis than Wolsey could have erected. Where Wolsey would have made the Crown independent of Parliament, Henry VIII. reduced Parliament to be a willing instrument of the royal will. Wolsey would have subverted the constitution, or at least would have reduced it to a lifeless form; Henry VIII. so worked the constitutional machinery that it became an additional source of power to his monarchy.

But though Wolsey was not successful in his method of making the royal power supreme over Parliament, he took the blame of failure upon himself, and saved the king's popularity. Wolsey's devotion to his master was complete, and cannot be assigned purely to selfish motives. Wolsey felt that his opinions, his policy, his aspirations had been formed through his intercourse with the king; and he was only strong when he and his master were thoroughly at one. At first the two men had been in complete agreement, and it cost Wolsey many a pang when he found that Henry did not entirely agree with his conclusions. After the imperial alliance was made Wolsey lost much of his brilliancy, his dash, and his force. This was not the result of age, or fatigue, or hopelessness so much as of the feeling that he and the king were no longer in accord. Like many other strong men, Wolsey was sensitive. He did not care for popularity, but he felt the need of being understood and trusted. He gave the king his affection, and he craved for a return.. There was no one else who could understand him or appreciate his aims, and when he felt that he was valued for his usefulness rather than trusted for what he was in himself, the spring of his life's energy was gone.

Still Wolsey laboured in all things to exalt the royal power, for in it he saw the only hope of the future, and England endorsed his opinion. But Wolsey was too great a man to descend to servility, and Henry always treated him with respect. In fact Wolsey always behaved with a strong sense of his personal dignity, and carried stickling for decorum to the verge of punctiliousness. Doubtless he had a decided taste for splendour and magnificence, but it is scarcely fair to put this down to the arrogance of an upstart, as was done by his English contemporaries. Wolsey believed in the influence of outward display on the popular mind, and did his utmost to throw over the king a veil of unapproachable grandeur and unimpeachable rectitude. He took upon himself the burden of the king's responsibilities, and stood forward to shield him against the danger of losing the confidence of his people. As the king's representative he assumed a royal state ; he wished men to see that they were governed from above, and he strove to accustom them to the pomp of power. In his missions abroad, and in his interviews with foreign ambassadors, he was still more punctilious than in the matters of domestic government. If the king was always to be regarded as the king, Wolsey, as the mouthpiece of the royal will, never abated his claims to honour only less than royal ; but he acted not so much from self-assertion as from policy. At home and abroad equally the greatness of the royal power was to be unmistakably set forth, and ostentation was an element in the game of brag to which a spirited foreign policy inevitably degenerates. It was for the king's sake that Wolsey magnified himself ; he never assumed an independent position, but all his triumphs were loyally laid at the king's feet. In this point, again, Wolsey overshot the mark, and did not understand the English people, who were not impressed in the manner which he intended. When Henry took the government more directly into his own hands he managed better for himself, for he knew how to identify the royal will with the aspirations of the people, and clothed his despotism with the appearance of paternal solicitude. He made the people think that he lived for them, and that their interests were his, whereas Wolsey endeavoured to convince the people that the king alone could guard their interests, and that their only course was to put entire confidence in him. Henry saw that men were easier to cajole than to convince; he worked for no system of royal authority, but contented himself with establishing his own will. In spite of the disadvantage of a royal education, Henry was a more thorough Englishman than Wolsey, though Wolsey sprang from the people.

It was Wolsey's teaching, however, that prepared Henry for his task. The king who could use a minister like Wolsey and then throw him away when he was no longer useful, felt that there was no limitation to his self-sufficiency.

Wolsey, indeed, was a minister in a sense which had never been seen in England before, for he held in his hand the chief power alike in Church and State. Not only was he chancellor, but also Archbishop of York, and endowed beside with special legatine powers. These powers were not coveted merely for purposes of show: Wolsey intended to use them, when opportunity offered, as a means of bringing the Church under the royal power as

completely as he wished to subject the State. He had
little respect for the ecclesiastical organisation as such ;
he saw its obvious weaknesses, and wished to provide a
remedy. If he was a candidate for the Papacy, it was
from no desire to pursue an ecclesiastical policy of his
own, but to make the papal power subservient to England's
interests. He was sufficiently clear-sighted to perceive
that national aspirations could not much longer be
repressed by the high-sounding claims of the Papacy ; he
saw that the system of the Church must be adapted to
the conditions of the time, and he wished to avert a
revolution by a quiet process of steady and reasonable
reform. He was perhaps honest in saying that he was
not greatly anxious for the Papacy ; for he knew that
England gave him ample scope for his energies, and he
hoped that the example of England would spread
throughout Europe. So at the beginning of his career
he pressed for legatine powers, which were grudgingly
granted by Leo X., first for one year, and afterwards
for five ; till the gratitude of Clement VII. conferred
them for life. Clothed with this authority, and working
in concert with the king, Wolsey was supreme over
the English Church, and perhaps dreamed of a future in
which the Roman Pontiff would practically resign his
claims over the northern churches to an English delegate,
who might become his equal or superior in actual power.

However this might be, he certainly contemplated the
reform of the English Church by means of a judicious
mixture of royal and ecclesiastical authority. Everything was propitious for such an undertaking, as the
position of the Church was felt to be in many ways
anomalous and antiquated. The rising middle class had

many grievances to complain of from the ecclesiastical courts; the new landlords looked with contempt on the management of monastic estates; the new learning mocked at the ignorance of the clergy, and scoffed at the superstitions of a simpler past which had survived unduly into an age when criticism was coming into fashion. The power of the Church had been great in days when the State was rude and the clergy were the natural leaders of men. Now the State was powerful and enjoyed men's confidence; they looked to the king to satisfy their material aspirations, and the Church had not been very successful in keeping their spiritual aspirations alive. It was not that men were opposed to the Church, but they judged its privileges to be excessive, its disciplinary courts to be vexatious, its officials to be too numerous, and its wealth to be devoted to purposes which had ceased to be of the first importance. There was a general desire to see a re-adjustment of many matters in which the Church was concerned; and before this popular sentiment churchmen found it difficult to assert their old pretensions, and preferred to rest contentedly under the protection of the Crown.

A trivial incident shows the general condition of affairs with sufficient clearness. One of the claims which on the whole the clergy had maintained was the right of trial before ecclesiastical courts; and the greater leniency of ecclesiastical sentences had been a useful modification of the severity of the criminal law, so that benefit of clergy had been permitted to receive large extension of interpretation. Further, the sanctity of holy places had been permitted to give rights of sanctuary to criminals fleeing from justice or revenge

. Both of these expedients had been useful in a rude state of society, and had done much to uphold a higher standard of humanity. But it was clear that they were only temporary expedients which were needless and even harmful as society grew more settled and justice was regularly administered. Henry VII. had felt the need of diminishing the rights of sanctuary, which gave a dangerous immunity to the numerous rebels against whom he had to contend, and he obtained a bull for that purpose from Pope Innocent VIII. The example which he set was speedily followed, and an Act was passed by the Parliament of 1511, doing away with sanctuary and benefit of clergy in the case of those who were accused of murder.

It does not seem that the Act met with any decided opposition at the time that it was passed; but there were still sticklers for clerical immunities, who regarded it as a dangerous innovation, and during the session of Parliament in 1515 the Abbot of Winchcombe preached a sermon in which he denounced it as an impious measure. Henry VIII. adopted a course which afterwards stood him in good stead in dealing with the Church; he submitted the question to a commission of divines and temporal peers. In the course of the discussion Standish, the Warden of the Friars Minors, put the point clearly and sensibly by saying, "The Act was not against the liberty of the Church, for it was passed for the weal of the whole realm." The clerical party were not prepared to face so direct an issue, and answered that it was contrary to the decretals. "So," replied Standish, "is the non-residence of bishops; yet that is common enough." Baffled in their appeal to law the bishops fell back upon Scripture, and quoted the text, "Touch not mine anointed." Again Standish turned against them the new critical spirit, which destroyed the old arguments founded on isolated texts. David, he said, used these words of all God's people as opposed to the heathen; as England was a Christian country the text covered the laity as well as the clergy. It was doubtless galling to the clerical party to be so remorselessly defeated by one of their own number, and their indignation was increased when the temporal lords on the commission decided against the Abbot of Winchcombe and ordered him to apologise.

The bishops vented their anger on Standish, and summoned him to answer for his conduct before Convocation, whereon he appealed to the king. Again Henry appointed a commission, this time exclusively of laymen, to decide between Standish and his accusers. They reported that Convocation, by its proceeding against one who was acting as a royal commissioner, had incurred the penalties of præmunire, and they added that the king could, if he chose, hold a parliament without the lords spiritual, who had no place therein save by virtue of their temporal possessions. Probably this was intended as a significant hint to the spirituality that they had better not interfere unduly with parliamentary proceedings. Moreover, at the same time a case had occurred which stirred popular feeling against the ecclesiastical courts. A London merchant had been arrested by the chancellor of the Bishop of London on a charge of heresy, and a few days after his arrest was found hanging dead in his cell. Doubtless the unhappy man had committed suicide, but there was a suspicion that his arrest was due to a private grudge on the part of the chancellor, who was accused of having made away with him privily. Popular feeling waxed high, and the lords who gave their decision so roundly against Convocation knew that they were sure of popular support.

Henry was not sorry of an opportunity of teaching the clergy their dependence upon himself, and he summoned the bishops before him that he might read them a lesson. Wolsey's action on this occasion is noticeable. He seems to have been the only one who saw the gravity of the situation, and he strove to effect a dignified compromise. Before the king could speak Wolsey knelt before him and interceded for the clergy. He said that they had designed nothing against the king's prerogative, but thought it their duty to uphold the rights of the Church; he prayed that the matter might be referred to the decision of the Pope. Henry answered that he was satisfied with the arguments of Standish. Fox, Bishop of Winchester, turned angrily on Standish, and Archbishop Warham plucked up his courage so far as to say feebly, "Many holy men have resisted the law of England on this point and have suffered martyrdom." But Henry knew that he had not to deal with a second Becket, and that the days of Becket had gone by for ever. He would have nothing to say to papal intervention or to clerical privilege; the time had come for the assertion of royal authority, and Henry could use his opportunity as skilfully as the most skilful priest. "We," said he, "are by God's grace king of England, and have no superior but God; we will maintain the rights of the Crown like our predecessors; your decrees you break and interpret at your pleasure:

but we will not consent to your interpretation any more
than our predecessors have done." The immemorial
rights of the English Crown were vaguer and more formidable than the rights of the Church, and the bishops
retired in silence. Henry did not forget the service
rendered him by Standish, who was made Bishop of St.
Asaph in 1518.

In this incident we have a forecast of the subsequent
course of events—the threat of præmunire, the assertion
of the royal supremacy, the submission of the clergy.
Nothing was wanting save a sufficient motive to work a
revolution in the ancient relations between Church and
State. Wolsey alone seems to have seen how precarious was the existing position of the Church. He knew
that the Church was wrong, and that it would have to
give way, but he wished to clothe its submission with a
semblance of dignity, and to use the papal power, not as
a means of guarding the rights of the Church, but as a
means of casting an air of ecclesiastical propriety over
their abandonment. Doubtless he proposed to use his
legatine power for that purpose if the need arose; but
he was loyal to the Church as an institution, and did not
wish it to fall unreservedly to the tender mercies of the
king. He saw that this was only to be avoided by a
judicious pliancy on the Church's part, which could gain
a breathing-space for carrying out gradual reforms.

The fact that Wolsey was a statesman rather than an
ecclesiastic gave him a clear view of the direction which
a conservative reformation should pursue. He saw that
the Church was too wealthy and too powerful for the
work which it was actually doing. The wealth and
power of the Church were a heritage from a former age,

in which the care for the higher interests of society fell
entirely into the hands of the Church because the State
was rude and barbarous, and had no machinery save for
the discharge of rudimentary duties. Bishops were the
only officials who could curb the lawlessness of feudal
lords; the clergy were the only refuge from local
tyranny; monks were the only landlords who cleared
the forests, drained the marshes, and taught the pursuits
of peace; monastery schools educated the sons of peasants, and the universities gave young men of ability a
career.   All the humanitarian duties of society were
discharged by the Church, and the Church had
grown in wealth and importance because of its readiness to discharge them.   But as the State grew
stronger, and as the power of Parliament increased, it
was natural that duties which had once been delegated
should be assumed by the community at large.   It was
equally natural that institutions which had once been
useful should outlast their usefulness and be regarded
with a jealous eye.   By the end of the reign of Edward
I. England had been provided with as many monastic
institutions as it needed, and the character of monasticism
began to decline.   Benefactions for social purposes from
that time forward were mainly devoted to colleges, hos-
pitals, and schools.   The fact that so many great churchmen were royal ministers shows how the energy of the
Church was placed at the disposal of the State and
was by it absorbed.   The Church possessed revenues,
and a staff of officials which were too large for the
time, in which it was not the only worker in the field of
social welfare.   It possessed rights and privileges which
were necessary for its protection in days of anarchy and

lawlessness, but which were invidious in days of more
settled government.   Moreover, the tenure of so much
land by ecclesiastical corporations like monasteries, was
viewed with jealousy in a time when commercial competition was becoming a dominant motive in a society
which had ceased to be mainly warlike.

From this point of view Wolsey was prepared for
gradual changes in the position of the Church; but he
did not wish those changes to be revolutionary, nor did
he wish them to be made by the power of the State.
He knew the real weakness of the Church and the practical omnipotence of the king; but he hoped to unite the
interests of the Crown and of the Church by his own
personal influence and by his position as the trusted
minister of king and Pope alike.

He did not, however, deceive himself about the practical difficulties in the way of a conservative reform,
which should remove the causes of popular discontent,
and leave the Church an integral part of the State
organisation.   He knew that the ecclesiastical system,
even in its manifest abuses, was closely interwoven with
English society, and he knew the strength of clerical
conservatism.   He knew also the dangers which beset
the Church if it came across the royal will and pleasure.
If any reform were to be carried out it must be by raising the standard of clerical intelligence.   Already many
things which had accorded with the simpler minds of an
earlier age had become objects of mockery to educated
laymen.   The raillery of Erasmus at the relics of St.
Thomas of Canterbury and the Virgin's milk preserved
at Walsingham expressed the difference which had arisen
between the old practices of religion and the belief of

thoughtful men. It would be well to divert some of the
revenues of the Church from the maintenance of idle and
ignorant monks to the education of a body of learned
clergy.

This diversion of monastic property had long been
projected and attempted. William of Wykeham endowed
his New College at Oxford with lands which he purchased
from monasteries. Henry VI. endowed Eton and
King's College with revenues which came from the suppression of alien priories. In 1497 John Alcock, Bishop
of Ely, obtained leave to suppress the decrepit nunnery
of St. Rhadegund in Cambridge and use its site for the
foundation of Jesus College. Wolsey only carried
farther and made more definite the example which had
previously been set when in 1524 he obtained from Pope
Clement VII. permission to convert into a college the
monastery of St. Frideswyde in Oxford. Soon after he
obtained a bull allowing him to suppress monasteries
with fewer than seven inmates, and devote their revenues
to educational purposes.

Nor was Wolsey the only man who was of opinion
that the days of monasticism were numbered. In 1515
Bishop Fox of Winchester contemplated the foundation
of a college at Oxford in connection with the monastery
of St. Swithin at Winchester. He was dissuaded from
making his college dependent on a monastery by his
brother bishop, Oldham of Exeter, who said, "Shall we
build houses and provide livelihoods for a company of
bussing monks, whose end and fall we ourselves may
live to see? No, no: it is meet to provide for the
increase of learning, and for such as by learning shall do
good to Church and commonwealth." Oldham's advice

prevailed, and the statutes of Fox's college of Brasenose were marked by the influence of the new learning as distinct from the old theology.

Still Wolsey's bull for the wholesale dissolution of small monasteries was the beginning of a process which did not cease till all were swept away. It introduced a principle of measuring the utility of old institutions and judging their right to exist by their power of rendering service to the community. Religious houses whose shrunken revenues could not support more than seven monks, according to the rising standard of monastic comfort, were scarcely likely to maintain serious discipline or pursue any lofty end. But it was the very reasonableness of this method of judgment which rendered it exceedingly dangerous. Tried by this standard, who could hope to escape? Fuller scarcely exaggerates when he says that this measure of Wolsey's "made all the forest of religious foundations in England to shake, justly fearing that the king would fell the oaks when the cardinal had begun to cut the underwood." It would perhaps have required too much wisdom for the monks to see that submission to the cardinal's pruning-knife was the only means of averting the clang of the royal axe.

The method which Wolsey pursued was afterwards borrowed by Henry VIII. Commissioners were sent out to inquire into the condition of small monasteries, and after an unfavourable report their dissolution was required, and their members were removed to a larger house. The work was one which needed care and dexterity as well as a good knowledge of business. Wolsey was lucky in his agents, chief amongst whom was Thomas Cromwell, an attorney whose cleverness Wolsey quickly perceived. In fact most of the men who so cleverly managed the dissolution of the monasteries for Henry had learned the knack under Wolsey, who was fated to train up instruments for purposes which he would have abhorred.

The immediate objects to which Wolsey devoted the money which he obtained by the dissolution of these useless monasteries were a college in his old university of Oxford and another in his native town of Ipswich. The two were doubtless intended to be in connection with one another, after the model of William of Wykeham's foundations at Winchester and Oxford, and those of Henry VI. at Eton and Cambridge. This scheme was never carried out in its integrity, for on Wolsey's fall his works were not completed, and were involved in his forfeiture. Few things gave him more grief than the threatened check of this memorial of his greatness, and owing to his earnest entreaties his college at Oxford was spared and was refounded. Its name, however, was changed from Cardinal College to Christ Church, and it was not entirely identified with Wolsey's glory. The college at Ipswich fell into abeyance.

Wolsey's design for Cardinal College was on a magnificent scale. He devised a large court surrounded by a cloister, with a spacious dining-hall on one side. The hall was the first building which he took in hand, and this fact is significant of his idea of academic life. He conceived a college as an organic society of men living in common, and by their intercourse generating and expressing a powerful body of opinion. Contemporaries mocked and said, " A fine piece of business; this car-

dinal projected a college and has built a tavern." They
did not understand that Wolsey was not merely adding
to the number of Oxford colleges, but was creating a
society which should dominate the University, and be
the centre of a new intellectual movement. For this
purpose Wolsey devised a foundation which should be at
once ecclesiastical and civil, and should set forward his
own conception of the relations between the Church and
the intellectual and social life of the nation. His foundation consisted of a dean, sixty canons, six professors,
forty petty canons, twelve chaplains, twelve clerks, and
sixteen choristers; and he proposed to fill it with men
of his own choice, who would find there a fitting sphere
for their energies.

Wolsey was a man well adapted to hold the balance
between the old and the new learning. He had been
trained in the theology of the schools, and was a student
of St. Thomas Aquinas; but he had learned by the
training of life to understand the new ideas; he grasped
their importance, and he foresaw their triumph. He
was a friend of the band of English scholars who brought
to Oxford the study of Greek, and he sympathised with
the intellectual aspirations of Grocyn, Colet, More, and
Erasmus. Perhaps he rather sympathised than understood; but his influence was cast on their side when the
opposition to the new learning broke out in the University and the Trojans waged a desperate and at first a
successful war against the Greeks. The more ignorant
among the clerical teachers objected to any widening of
the old studies, and resented the substitution of biblical
or patristic theology for the study of the schoolmen.
They dreaded the effects of the critical method, and were

not reassured when Grocyn, in a sermon at St. Paul's Cathedral, declared that the writings attributed to Dionysius the Areopagite were spurious. A wave of obscurantism swept over Oxford, and, as Tyndale puts it, "the barking curs, Dun's disciples, the children of darkness, raged in every pulpit against Greek, Latin, and Hebrew." Wolsey used the king's authority to rebuke the assailants of learning, but the new teachers withdrew from Oxford, and Wolsey saw that if the new learning was to make way it must have a secure footing. Accordingly he set himself to get the universities into his power, and in 1517 proposed to found university lectureships in Oxford. Hitherto the teaching given in the universities had been voluntary; teachers arose and maintained themselves by a process of natural selection. Excellent as such a system may seem, it did not lead to progress, and already the Lady Margaret, Countess of Richmond, Henry VII's mother, had adopted the advice of Bishop Fisher, and founded divinity professorships in the two universities. Wolsey wished to extend this system and organise an entire staff of teachers for university purposes. We do not know how far he showed his intention, but such was his influence that Oxford submitted its statutes to him for revision. Wolsey's hands were too full of other work for him to undertake at once so delicate a matter; but he meant undoubtedly to reorganise the system of university education, and for this purpose prevailed on Cambridge also to entrust its statutes to his hands. Again he had prepared the way for a great undertaking, and had dexterously used his position to remove all obstacles, and prepare a field for the work of reconstruction. Again he was

L

prevented from carrying out his designs, and his educational reform was never actually made. We can only trace his intentions in the fact that he brought to Oxford a learned Spaniard, Juan Luis Vives, to lecture on rhetoric, and we may infer that he intended to provide both universities with a staff of teachers chosen from the first scholars of Europe.

Another matter gives another indication of Wolsey's desire to remove the grievances felt against the Church. If the monasteries were survivals of a time when the Church discharged the humanitarian duties of society, the ecclesiastical courts were in a like manner survivals of a time when the civil courts were not yet able to deal with many points which concerned the relations between man and man, or which regulated individual conduct. Thus marriage was a religious ceremony, and all questions which arose from the marriage contract were decided in the ecclesiastical courts. Similarly wills were recognised by the Church, as resting on the moral basis of mutual confidence, long before the State was prepared to acknowledge their validity. Besides these cases which arose from contract, the Church exercised a disciplinary supervision over its members for the good of their souls, and to avoid scandals in a Christian community. On all these points the principles of the Church had leavened the conceptions of the State, and the civil jurisdiction had in many matters overtaken the ecclesiastical. But the clerical courts stood stubbornly upon their claim to greater antiquity, and the activity of ecclesiastical lawyers found plenty of work to do. Disciplinary jurisdiction was unduly extended by a class of trained officials, and was resented by the growing independence of the rising middle class. No doubt the ecclesiastical courts needed reform, but the difficulties in the way of reforming legal procedure are always great. Wolsey faced the problem in a way which is most characteristic of his statesmanship. He strove to bring the question to maturity for solution by getting the control of the ecclesiastical courts into his own hands. For this purpose he used his exceptional position as Papal Legate, and instituted a legatine court which should supersede the ordinary jurisdiction. Naturally enough this brought him into collision with Archbishop Warham, and his fall prevented him from developing his policy. His attempt only left the ecclesiastical courts in worse confusion, and added to the strength of the opposition, which soon robbed them of most of their powers. It added also to Wolsey's unpopularity, and gave a shadow of justice to the unworthy means which were used for his destruction.

In fact, wherever we look, we see that in domestic affairs Wolsey had a clear conception of the objects to be immediately pursued by a conservative reformer. But a conservative reformer raises as much hostility as does a revolutionist, for the mass of men are not sufficiently foreseeing or sufficiently disinterested willingly to abandon profitable abuses. They feel less animosity against the open enemy who aims avowedly at their destruction, than against the seeming friends who would deprive them of what they consider to be their rights. The clergy submitted more readily to the abolition of their privileges by the king than they would have submitted to a reform at the hands of Wolsey. They could understand the one; they could not understand the other

This was natural, for Wolsey had no lofty principles to set before them ; he had only the wisdom of a keen-sighted statesman, who read the signs of the times. Indeed he did not waste his time in trying to persuade others to see with his eyes. He could not have ventured to speak out and say that the Church must choose between the tender mercies of the royal power and submission to the discretion of one who, standing between the king and the Pope, was prepared to throw a semblance of ecclesiastical recognition over reforms which were inevitable. It is clear that Wolsey was working for the one possible compromise, and he hoped to effect it by his own dexterity. Secure of the royal favour, secure through his political importance of the papal acquiescence in the use which he made of his legatine power, standing forward as the chief ecclesiastic in England, he aimed at accomplishing such reforms as would have brought into harmony the relations between Church and State. He did not hope to do this by persuasion, but by power, and had taken steps to lay his hand cautiously on different parts of the ecclesiastical organisation. With this idea before him we may safely acquit Wolsey of any undue ambition for the papal office ; he doubted whether his influence would be increased or not by its possession.

In everything that Wolsey did he played for the highest stakes, and risked all upon the hope of ultimate success. He trusted to justify himself in the long-run, and was heedless of the opposition which he called forth. Resting solely upon the royal favour, he did not try to conciliate, nor did he pause to explain. Men could not understand his ends, but they profoundly disliked his means. The suppression of small monasteries, which might be useless but served to provide for younger sons or dependants of country families, was very unpopular, as coming from a cardinal who enjoyed the revenues of many ecclesiastical offices whose duties he did not discharge. The setting up of a legatine court was hateful to the national sentiment of Englishmen, who saw in it only another engine of ecclesiastical oppression. The pomp and magnificence wherewith Wolsey asserted a greatness which he mainly valued as a means of doing his country service, was resented as the vulgar arrogance of an upstart. Wolsey's ideas were too great to pay any heed to the prejudices of Englishmen which, after all, have determined the success of all English ministers, and which no English statesman has ever been powerful enough to disregard.

CHAPTER IX

IF Wolsey hoped that the peace with France, which he had so successfully concluded in the beginning of 1527, would enable him to reassert England's influence on the Continent, and would give him an opportunity for the work of domestic reform, he was sorely disappointed. A new matter arose, not entirely unexpected, but which widened into unexpected issues, and consumed Wolsey's energies till it led to his fall. The project of the king's divorce was suddenly mooted; and this personal matter, before it was ripe for settlement, gradually drew into its sphere all the questions concerning England's foreign and domestic policy which Wolsey's statesmanship had been trying to solve by wise and well-considered means. Wolsey had been gathering into his hands the threads of a complicated policy, each one of which required dexterous handling, in accordance with a great design. He found himself suddenly called upon to act precipitately for the accomplishment of a small matter, which brought all the difficulties of his position prominently forward, and gave him no time for that skilful diplomacy in

which he excelled. Moreover, when the project was
started neither Henry nor Wolsey could have foreseen
the complications which would arise ; still less could
Wolsey have known the obstinacy which the faintest
opposition to the royal will would develop in the king,
or the extent to which he could persuade himself that
the satisfaction of the royal pleasure was the sole purpose
of the existence of the power of the State. At first
Henry had sympathised with Wolsey's far-reaching
schemes.   Latterly he had at all events been willing to
allow Wolsey to have his own way on the whole. The
time came when he showed himself a hard taskmaster,
and demanded that Wolsey should at all costs satisfy his
personal desires in a matter which he persuaded himself
was all-important to the nation at large.

Viewed according to the general notions of the time,
there was nothing very surprising in the fact that Henry
VIII. should wish for a divorce.   Royal marriages were
made and unmade from motives of expediency ; it was
only a question of obtaining a decent plea.   The sons
of Katharine had died in infancy, and Mary was the only
heir of the English throne ; it was a matter of importance
to the future of England that the succession to the
throne should be clearly established.   If Henry had
remained attached to his wife this consideration would
not have been put forward ; but Henry was never famed
for constancy.   He was in the prime of life, while
Katharine was over forty.   He had developed in character, not for the better, while she remained true to the
narrow traditions of her early training.   She was an
excellent housewife, conscientious, decorous, and capable ;
but she was devoted to the political interests of Spain,

and admired her nephew Charles. While the imperial
alliance was warmly pursued by Henry she was
happy; when Henry's zeal for Charles began to
fade she felt offended, and was not judicious in the
display of her political bias. Henry was more and more
annoyed by his wife's discontent, and the breach between
them rapidly widened. When Henry broke with
Charles and allied himself with France he seems to
have felt that his domestic peace was at an end, and he
was not the man to shrink from the effort to re-establish
it upon another basis.

Perhaps none of these considerations would have
moved Henry to take prompt action if his desires
had not been kindled by a new object of his affection.
He had not been a faithful husband, and Katharine seems
to have been indulgent to his infidelities. In the course
of 1526 he was captivated by the charms of Anne Boleyn,
as he had formerly been captivated by her sister Mary.
But Anne had learned that the king was fickle, and she
resolved that she would not be so easily won as to be
lightly abandoned. She skilfully managed to make herself agreeable to the king till his passion for her became
so violent that he was prepared to accept her terms and
make her his lawful wife.

Wolsey was not in favour of this plan; but he was
not opposed to getting rid of the political influence
of Katharine, and he believed that the king's fancy
for Anne Boleyn would rapidly pass away. Whatever
his own personal opinion might be, he did not venture
to gainsay the king in a matter on which he was resolved,
and he lent himself to be an instrument in a matter
which involved him in measures which became more and

more discreditable. The first idea of the king was to
declare his marriage with Katharine unlawful, on the
ground that she had previously been his brother's wife ;
but he was cognisant of that when he married her and
had applied for a papal dispensation to remedy that
source of invalidity. Doubtless some plea might be
discovered to enable the Pope to set aside the dispensation granted by his predecessor. But whatever technical
grounds might be used to justify the Pope's decision in
the king's favour, the Pope could not be expected to act
in such a manner as to offend the Powers of Europe and
shock the moral sense of Englishmen. Wolsey did not
hide from himself that there were three hindrances in
the way of legalising the king's divorce. The opinion
of England was not in its favour ; Charles V. was likely
to resent the affront which it would put upon his aunt,
and the Pope could not afford to alienate one who was
becoming all-powerful in Italy that he might win the
distant friendship of the English king ; Francis I. had
just made a treaty with Henry VIII., by which the hand
of Mary had been promised to his son, and he was not
likely to wish to see Mary declared to be illegitimate.
These were serious elements of opposition, which it
would require considerable skill to overcome.

The first measure which suggested itself to Henry and
Wolsey was to put the king's plea into shape, and endorse
it with the authority of the English Church. For this
purpose a suit was secretly instituted against the king
in Wolsey's legatine court. Henry was solemnly informed that a complaint had been made to Wolsey, as
censor of public morals, that he had cohabited for
eighteen years with his brother's wife. Henry consented

that Archbishop Warham should be joined with Wolsey as assessor, and named a proctor who should plead his cause. Three sessions of this court were held with the profoundest secrecy in May; but in spite of all the attempts at secrecy the imperial ambassador discovered what was going on. The object of this procedure seems to have been to produce a sentence from the legate's court in England which should be confirmed by the Pope without right of appeal. If the Pope had been a free agent he might conceivably have adopted this course; but the news soon reached England that Rome had been sacked by Bourbon, and that the Pope was trembling before Charles V. In this turn of affairs it was useless to proceed farther on the supposition that he would unhesitatingly comply with the wishes of Henry and Wolsey. A court sitting in secret would have no influence on English opinion, and Wolsey proposed that its sittings should be suspended, and the opinions of the English bishops be taken as a means of educating public opinion.

But Katharine had been informed of the king's intentions concerning her, and showed a purpose of defending her rights. It would be very awkward if she were the first to make the matter public, and were to appeal to the Pope or her kinsman Charles. The question would then become a political question, and Henry was not prepared with allies. So on 22d June the king broached his difficulties to Katharine. He told her of his scruples, and of his intentions of submitting them to the decision of canonists and theologians; meanwhile they had · better live apart. Katharine burst into tears, and the king vaguely tried to assure her that all was being done for the best, and begged her to keep the matter secret. His only object was to prevent her from taking any open steps till he had assured himself of the countenance of the French king to his plans. For this purpose Wolsey was sent on an embassy, ostensibly to settle some questions raised by the French treaty, really to concert with Francis I. a scheme for bringing to bear upon the Pope a pressure which should be strong enough to counteract the influence of Charles V. So, on 3d July, Wolsey left London on his last diplomatic mission. Men who saw Wolsey set out with more than his accustomed state, escorted by nine hundred horsemen, thought, doubtless, that the cardinal's greatness was as high as ever; but those who watched more closely saw him in the splendid ceremonial of the Church of Canterbury "weep very tenderly," for his mind was ill at ease. He must have felt that he was going to use his talents for a bad end, and that all patriotism and nobility had vanished from his aim. On his way to Dover he had a conference with Archbishop Warham, whom he instructed about the conduct to be observed towards the queen. Then at Rochester he sounded Bishop Fisher, the most holy and upright of the English bishops, who had already been asked by Katharine to give her counsel, though she had not ventured to tell him what was the subject on which she wished for his advice. So Wolsey told his own story; that the king's conscience was disquiet, and that he wished to have his scruples set at rest by the opinions of learned men. He represented that Katharine by her hastiness was throwing difficulties in the way of the king's considerate procedure, and threatened to publish the matter, and so create an open scandal. Fisher believed Wolsey's tale, and was beguiled into a belief of the king's good intentions, which the queen could not understand. About the validity of Henry's marriage Wolsey could not get from Fisher an opinion contrary to the authority of a papal dispensation; but he contrived to alienate Fisher from sympathy with Katharine, and so left the queen without a friend while he proceeded to machinate against her in France.

We have from one of Wolsey's attendants, George Cavendish, his gentleman - usher, a full account of Wolsey's journey in France. On one point he gives us valuable insight into Wolsey's character where Wolsey has been much misrepresented. He tells us how at Calais he summoned his attendants and addressed them about their behaviour. He explained that the services which he required from them were not personal but official, and his words were those of a statesman who understood, but did not over-estimate, the value of external things. "Ye shall understand," he said, "that the king's majesty, upon certain weighty considerations, hath for the more advancement of his royal dignity assigned me in this journey to be his lieutenant-general, and what reverence belongeth to the same I will tell you. That for my part I must, by virtue of my commission of lieutenantship, assume and take upon me, in all honours and degrees, to have all such service and reverence as to his highness's presence is meet and due, and nothing thereof to be neglected or omitted by me that to his royal estate is appurtenant. And for my part, ye shall see me that I will not omit one jot thereof." Then he added some wise advice

about the courtesies to be observed in their intercourse
with the French.

When matters of etiquette had thus been arranged,
Wolsey rode out of Calais on 22d July, and pursued his
journey to Abbeville, where he awaited the arrival of
Francis I. at Amiens. On 4th August he entered Amiens,
and was received with royal honours. His interviews
with Francis and the queen-mother were most satis-
factory on matters of general policy: the English
alliance was firmly accepted, and all questions between
the two Crowns were in a fair way towards settlement
Wolsey waited till the political alliance was firmly established before he broached the personal matter of the
divorce. Meanwhile he meditated on the schemes which
might be pursued by the allied kings to satisfy
Henry's desires. He proposed that they should join in
demanding from Charles V. that he should restore the
Pope's independence, in the hope that the Pope when
freed from constraint would be willing to show his
gratitude by complying with Henry's demands. If
they failed in procuring the Pope's release, they should
declare the papal power to be in abeyance, and summon
the cardinals to meet at Avignon, where, under Wolsey's
presidency, they should transact such business as the
Pope in his captivity was unable to discharge.

Either of these methods was technically decorous;
but they did not much commend themselves to Henry
VIII., whose passion for Anne Boleyn daily increased,
and who was impatient of any procedure that involved
delay. So Henry listened coldly to Wolsey's proposals
for a "sure, honourable, and safe" termination of the
"king's matter," as the divorce was now called: he

wished for a " good and brief conclusion," and gave ear
to the advice of Anne Boleyn and her friends. It was
easy for them to point out that Wolsey was an old-
fashioned statesman, full of prejudice where the Church
was concerned. They urged that the king could do
better for himself, and could deal more expeditiously
with the Pope than could a churchman who was bound
to adopt a humble attitude towards his ecclesiastical
superior. So Henry determined to take the matter
into his own hands, and send his secretary Knight to
negotiate with the Pope without Wolsey's intervention.

Wolsey, meanwhile, in ignorance of the King's intentions, but distressed at the difficulties which he foresaw,
followed the French Court to Compiegne, where he
divided his time between diplomatic conflicts, festivities,
and the despatch of business. One morning, Cavendish
tells us, " He rose early about four of the clock, sitting
down to write letters into England unto the king, commanding one of his chaplains to prepare him to mass,
insomuch that the said chaplain stood revested until
four of the clock at afternoon ; all which season my
lord never rose once even to eat any meat, but continually wrote his letters, with his own hands, having all
that time his nightcap and kerchief on his head. And
about the hour of four of the clock, at afternoon, he
made an end of writing, and commanded one Christopher
Gunner, the king's servant, to prepare him without
delay to ride empost into England with his letters,
whom he despatched away or ever he drank. And that
done he went to mass, and said his other divine service
with his chaplain, as he was accustomed to do ; and then
went straight into a garden ; and after he had walked

the space of an hour or more, and said his evensong, he went to dinner and supper all at once; and making a small repast, he went to his bed, to take his rest for the night."

While Wolsey was thus labouring in this thorny matter, he received a visit from Knight on his way to Rome. Knight's instructions were to demand from the Pope a dispensation for Henry to marry again before the divorce from Katharine had been pronounced; failing this, to marry immediately after his marriage with Katharine was declared invalid. Further, he was to ask the Pope to issue a bull delegating his spiritual authority to Cardinal Wolsey during his captivity. No doubt this was an expeditious way to cut existing difficulties; but it was too expeditious to suit the traditions of the Papal Court. Its obvious clumsiness showed that it was not the work of Wolsey's hand; and it was unwise for the king to inform the Pope that he was trying to act without Wolsey's knowledge.

Though Wolsey was left in ignorance of the nature of Knight's instructions, he could not but suspect that the king was acting without his full knowledge. He finished his work at Compiegne and returned to England at the end of September. He at once repaired to the Court at Richmond, and sent to tell the king of his arrival. Hitherto the king had always retired to a private room when he received the cardinal alone. Now Anne Boleyn was with the king in the great hall, and scarcely had Wolsey's message been delivered than she broke in, "Where else should the cardinal come than here where the king is?" The king confirmed her command, and Wolsey found himself ushered

into the hall, where Henry sat amusing himself with
Anne and his favourites.   Serious talk was out of the
question.   Wolsey was no longer first in the king's
confidence.   He went away feeling that Anne Boleyn
was his political rival, whom he could only overcome by
serving better than she could serve herself.   Henceforth
he had two masters instead of one, and he did not deceive
himself that the continuance of his power depended
solely on his usefulness in the matter of the divorce.

As Wolsey showed himself compliant, Anne Boleyn
treated him graciously while she waited to hear the
result of Knight's mission to Rome.   It was not easy
for him to enter the city, which was in possession of the
Spaniards, and when he entered it he could not hold
any personal communication with Clement VII., who was
shut up in the Castle of St. Angelo.   On 9th December
Clement escaped to Orvieto, where Knight soon joined
him, and showed his incapacity for the work which had
been confided to him by revealing to the papal officials
the whole details of the matter, which he ought to
have kept secret.   Clement saw at once the value of
Henry's conscientious scruples, and learned that he was
moved solely by a desire to marry Anne Boleyn, a
connection which could not be excused by any paramount
reasons of political expediency.   However anxious the
Pope might be to oblige the English king, there were
limits to his complacency, and Knight had not the wits
to cast a fair appearance over a disgraceful matter.   Yet
Clement did not wish to offend Henry by refusing
his request at once.   The demand for a dispensation
empowering the king to marry at once had already
been dropped at Wolsey's instance.   Knight carried

with him a form of dispensation allowing Henry to marry as soon as his marriage with Katharine was dissolved. This form was amended by one of the cardinals, and was signed by the Pope. Knight started back to England, convinced that he had done his business excellently, and was bearing to the king the permission which he desired.

When the documents were placed in Wolsey's hands he saw at once that they were worthless. What Henry wanted was permission for Wolsey to decide the question in the Pope's behalf, and permission for himself to act at once as soon as Wolsey's decision was pronounced The documents which he received did not bar Katharine's right of appeal; consequently Wolsey's decision would be of no effect, and the king could not lawfully marry again pending the appeal. In fact, the Pope reserved the entire decision of the matter in his own hand.

It was a small matter for Wolsey to triumph over a man like Knight; but Knight's failure showed Henry and Anne Boleyn that they must put their confidence in Wolsey after all. So in February 1528 Wolsey had to begin again from the beginning, and had to undo the mischief which Knight's bungling had made. He chose as his agents his secretary, Stephen Gardiner, and Edward Foxe, one of the king's chaplains. They were instructed to ask that the Pope would join with Wolsey some special legate, and give them power to pronounce a final judgment. For this purpose they were to plead Henry's cause with all earnestness, and say that the king was moved only by the scruples of his conscience; at the same time they were to praise the virtues of Anne

M

Boleyn, and say that the king was solely moved by considerations of his duty to his country in his desire to marry her. Further, they were to insist on the dishonour which would be done to the Holy See if the Pope, through fear of Charles V., were to refuse to do justice. If the king could not obtain justice from the Pope he would be compelled to seek it elsewhere, and live outside the laws of Holy Church; and however reluctant, he would be driven to this for the quiet of his conscience.

Truly these pleas were sorely contradictory. Henry was ready to acknowledge to the fullest extent the papal power of granting dispensations, and was ready to submit to the justice of the Pope as the highest justice upon earth. But this was solely on condition that the Pope gave decision according to his wishes. He regarded the Papacy as an excellent institution so long as it was on his own side. If it refused to see the justice of his pleas, then he fell back as strenuously as did Luther on the necessity of satisfying his own conscience, and to do so he was ready, if need were, to break with the Church. Truly the movement in Germany had affected public opinion more than was supposed when Wolsey could hold such language to the Pope. He did not know what a terrible reality that curious conscience of Henry would become. His words were a truer prophecy than he dreamed.

However, this line of argument was stubbornly pursued by Gardiner even in the Pope's presence. Clement at Orvieto was not surrounded by the pomp and splendour customary to his office. The English envoys found him in a little room, seated on a wooden bench which was covered with "an old coverlet not worth twenty pence." But he did not see his way to a restoration of his dignity by an unhesitating compliance with the demands of the English king; on the other hand, the mere fact that his fortunes had sunk so low demanded greater circumspection. He was not likely to escape from dependence on Charles V. by making himself the tool of Francis I. and Henry VIII.; such a proceeding would only lead to the entire destruction of the papal authority. Its restoration must be achieved by holding the balance between the opposing Powers of Europe, and Henry VIII.'s desire for a divorce gave the Pope an opportunity of showing that he was still a personage of some importance. Dynastic questions still depended on his decree, and he could use Henry's application as a means of showing Charles that he had something to fear from the Papacy, and that it was his policy to make the Papacy friendly to himself. So Clement resolved to adopt a congenial course of temporising, in the hope that he might see his advantage in some turn of affairs. No doubt he thought that Henry's matter would soon settle itself; either his passion for Anne Boleyn would pass away, or he would make her his mistress. The stubbornness of Henry, his strange hold upon formal morality while pursuing an immoral course of conduct, his imperious self-will, which grew by opposition—these were incalculable elements which might have upset the plans of wiser men than Clement VII.

So the Pope acted the part of the good simple man who wishes to do what is right. He lamented his own ignorance, and proposed to consult those who were more learned in canon law than himself. When Gardiner

said that England asked nothing but justice, and if it
were refused would be driven to think that God had taken
away from the Holy See the key of knowledge, and
would begin to adopt the opinion of those who thought
that pontifical laws, which were not clear to the
Pope himself, might well be committed to the flames,
Clement sighed, and suggested a compromise. Then he
added, with a smile, that though canonists said "the
Pope has all laws in the cabinet of his breast," yet God
had not given him the key to open that cabinet; he
could only consult his cardinals.

Gardiner's outspoken remonstrances were useless
against one who pleaded an amiable incompetence.
Against the churnings of Henry's conscience Clement
set up the churnings of his own conscience, and no
one could gainsay the Pope's right to a conscience as
much as the English king. After pursuing this course
during the month of March the Pope at length with
sighs and tears devised a compromise, in which he feared
that he had outstepped the bounds of discretion. He
accepted one of the documents which the English envoys
had brought, the permission for the king to marry whom
he would as soon as his marriage with Katharine had
been dissolved. He altered the terms of the other
document, which provided for the appointment of a commission with plenary powers to pronounce on the validity
of the king's marriage; he granted the commission, but
did not give it plenary power; at the same time he chose
as the commissioner who was to sit with Wolsey Cardinal
Campeggio, who was the protector of England in the
Papal Court, and who was rewarded for his services by
holding the bishopric of Hereford. In this way he

showed every mark of goodwill to Henry short of ac-
quiescing entirely in the procedure which he proposed;
but he kept the final decision of the matter in his own
hands.

Gardiner was not wholly pleased with this result of
his skill and firmness : after all his efforts to obtain a
definite solution the Pope had managed to escape from
giving any binding promise.   Still, Foxe put a good
face on Gardiner's exploits when he returned to England
in the end of April.   Henry and Anne Boleyn were
delighted, and Wolsey, though he was more dissatisfied
than Gardiner, thought it best to be hopeful.   He tried
to bind the Pope more firmly, and instructed Gardiner
to press that the law relating to Henry's case should be
laid down in a papal decretal, so that the legates should
only have to determine the question of fact ; this decretal
he promised to keep entirely secret; besides this, he urged
that there should be no delay in sending Campeggio.

During these months of expectancy Wolsey conde-
scended to ingratiate himself with Anne Boleyn, who had
become a political personage of the first importance.
Anne was sure of Wolsey's devotion to her interests so
long as they were also the king's, and could not dispense
with Wolsey's skill.   So she was kindly, and wrote
friendly letters to Wolsey, and asked for little gifts of
tunny-fish and shrimps.   The English Court again
resembled an amiable family party, whose members
were all of one mind.   In the course of the summer
they were all thrown into terror by an outbreak
of the "Sweating Sickness," which devastated the
country.   Anne Boleyn was attacked, though not
severely ; and Henry showed that his devotion to her

did not proceed to the length of risking his own precious life for her sake. He fled to Waltham, and Anne was left with her father; Henry protested by letter his unalterable affection, but kept out of harm's way till all risk of infection was past. At the same time he showed great solicitude for Wolsey's health, as did also Anne Boleyn. It seemed as though Wolsey were never more useful or more highly esteemed.

Yet, strangely enough, this outbreak of the plague drew upon Wolsey the most significant lesson which he had yet received of his own real position and of Henry's resoluteness to brook no check upon his royal will. Amongst others who perished in the sickness was the Abbess of Wilton, and Anne Boleyn wished that the vacant office should be given to one of the nuns of the abbey, Eleanor Carey, sister of William Carey, who had married Anne's sister Mary. Wolsey was informed of the wishes of Anne and of the king on this point; but on examination found that Eleanor's life and character were not such as to fit her for the office. He therefore proposed to confer it on the prioress, Isabella Jordan. It would seem, however, that Eleanor's friends were determined to efface in some degree the scandal which their unwise haste had occasioned, and they retaliated by spreading reports injurious to the character of the prioress. Wolsey did not believe these reports; but Anne Boleyn and the king agreed that if their nominee was to be set aside, the cardinal's nominee should be set aside likewise, and Wolsey was informed of the king's decision. Perhaps Wolsey failed to understand the secret motives which were at work; perhaps he had so far committed himself before receiving the king's mes

sage that he could not well go back ; perhaps he consci-
entiously did what he thought right. Anyhow, he
appointed Isabella Jordan, and sent her appointment to
the king for confirmation ; further, he gave as his excuse
that he had not understood the king's will in the matter.

To his extreme surprise and mortification the king
took the opportunity thus afforded of reading him a
lecture on his presumption, and reminding him that he
was expected to render implicit obedience. Matters
were no longer arranged between Henry and Wolsey
alone ; Anne Boleyn was a third party, and the king's
pride was engaged in showing her that his word was
law. When Henry took his pen in hand he assumed
the mantle of royal dignity, and he now gave Wolsey a
sample of the royal way of putting things which was so
effectual in his later dealings with his Parliament. He
began by assuring Wolsey that the great love he bore
him led him to apply the maxim, "Whom I love I
chasten ;" he spoke therefore not in displeasure but for
Wolsey's good. He could not but be displeased that
Wolsey had acted contrary to his orders ; he was the
more displeased that Wolsey had pleaded ignorance as
an excuse for his disobedience. He overwhelmed him
with quotations from his letters on the subject, and went
on, "Ah, my lord, it is a double offence both to do ill
and colour it too; but with men that have wit it cannot be
accepted so. Wherefore, good my lord, use no more that
way with me, for there is no man living that more hateth
it." He then went on to tell Wolsey that there were many
rumours current about the means which he was employing to raise money from religious houses for the foundation of his new colleges ; he told him this because "I

dare be bolder with you than many that mumble it
abroad." He showed that he had not forgotten the
refusal of the monasteries to help in the Amicable
Grant: why should they now give money to Wolsey unless they had some interested motive in doing so? He
advised Wolsey to look closely into the matter, and
ended, "I pray you, my lord, think not that it is upon
any displeasure that I write this unto you. For surely
it is for my discharge afore God, being in the room that
I am in; and secondly, for the great zeal I bear unto
you, not undeserved on your behalf. Wherefore, I
pray you, take it so; and I assure you, your fault
acknowledged, there shall remain in me no spark of displeasure; trusting hereafter you shall recompense that
with a thing much more acceptable to me."

This letter came upon Wolsey as a sudden revelation
of his true position. It showed him the reality of all the
vague doubts and fears which he had for some time been
striving to put from him. He was crushed into abject-
ness, which he did not even strive to conceal from others.
He took the immediate matters of complaint seriously
to heart, and wished to annul the appointment of Isabella Jordan, which the king ruled to be unnecessary;
on that point he was satisfied with having asserted a
principle. But he advised Wolsey to receive no more
gifts for his colleges from religious houses, and Wolsey
promised not to do so. "Thereby I trust, nor by any
other thing hereafter unlawfully taken, your poor
cardinal's conscience shall not be spotted, encumbered,
or entangled; purposing, with God's help and your
gracious favour, so to order the rest of my poor life that
it shall appear to your Highness that I love and dread

God and also your Majesty." This was a lamentable prostration of the moral authority of the chief churchman in England before the king, and showed Wolsey's weakness. He knew that he had not demeaned himself as befitted his priestly office ; and though he may have felt that no man in England had less right than the king to reprove his conduct on moral grounds, still he could not plead that he was above reproach. In the particular matter of which he was accused—extorting money from the religious houses in return for immunities granted in virtue of his legatine power—there is no evidence that Wolsey was guilty. But he could not say that he had a conscience void of offence ; he had acted throughout his career as a statesman and a man of the world. If the king chose to hold him up to moral reprobation he had no valid defence to offer. He had disregarded the criticisms of others that he might serve the king more faithfully ; but if the king took upon himself the office of critic he had nothing to urge. It was because Henry had taken the measure of churchmen such as Wolsey that he ventured in later times to hold such lofty language in addressing the clergy. Henry was always superior to the weakness of imagining that his own conduct needed any defence, or his own motives any justification.

Wolsey, though forgiven with royal graciousness, was profoundly depressed, and could not recover his sense of security. The future was to him big with menaces, and perhaps he looked most sadly upon his designs which yet remained unrealised. He saw that his activity must henceforth work in a smaller sphere, and that he must make haste to finish what he had on hand The ugly business of the divorce looked to him still uglier

Either he would fail in his efforts to move the Pope, in which case he lost his hold upon the king at once, or, if he succeeded, he saw that the reign of Anne Boleyn meant the end of his own uncontested influence. The king's letter was at least significant of that : he would never have raised a question about so trivial a matter if he had not wished to justify his absolute power in the eyes of one who was to him all-important.

So Wolsey faced the future; he put his aspirations on a lower level, and wished only to garner certainly some of the fruits of his life-long labour. He told the French ambassador, Du Bellay, "that if God permitted him to see the hatred of these two nations (France and England) extinguished, and firm amity established, as he hopes it will shortly be, with a reform of the laws and customs of the country, such as he would effect if peace were made, and the succession of the kingdom assured, especially if this marriage took place, and an heir male were born of it, he would at once retire, and serve God for the rest of his life ; and that, without any doubt, on the first honourable occasion he could find, he would give up politics." Doubtless Wolsey was genuine in these utterances, and felt that he was resigning much when he reduced his designs within the limits which he here set forth. But limited as they were, they still contained an entire scheme for the reconstruction of English politics. Wolsey's plans remained complete, however much he might be willing to reduce them ; he was incapable of being a mere attendant upon chance.

For the present he was awaiting with growing anxiety the coming of Cardinal Campeggio, which was delayed, according to the Pope's policy of procrastination. First the cardinal had to contend against the difficulties created by the disorderly state of Italy ; then he was delayed by an attack of the gout, which made his movements slow ; and he did not reach London till 8th October. When he came he was not prepared to act at once, nor did he treat Wolsey as an equal but rather as a subordinate in the work of the commission. In fact, Campeggio behaved as judge, and Wolsey as the king's advocate. Campeggio's instructions were first to try and persuade the king to lay aside his purpose of a divorce. He soon saw that this was useless, and Wolsey plainly warned him with prophetic instinct. " Most reverend lord, beware lest, in like manner as the greater part of Germany, owing to the harshness and severity of a certain cardinal, has become estranged from the Apostolic See and the faith, it should be said that another cardinal has given the same occasion to England, with the same result."

Failing to shake the king's determination, the next course which Campeggio was ordered to pursue was to persuade the queen to comply with the king's wishes. Katharine was still treated with outward respect, but was cut off from all friends and advisers, and subjected to a secret and galling persecution. Still she maintained a resolute spirit, and withstood the pleadings of Wolsey and Campeggio, who urged her to give way and withdraw to a monastery, for the quieting of the king's conscience. Katharine replied that there was nothing of which his conscience need be afraid, and that she intended " to live and die in the estate of matrimony to which God had called her." The obstinacy of Katharine was as invincible as the obstinacy of Henry ; and Katharine had right on her side

Nothing remained save for the legates to proceed to the trial of the case; and in the trial Campeggio's instructions bade him procrastinate to the utmost in hopes the king might give way before the long delay. Wolsey had foreseen this possibility when he demanded that Campeggio should bring with him a decretal defining the law as applicable to the case. This decretal Campeggio was instructed to show the king, but keep in his own hands, so that it was useless for Wolsey's purpose. His first object was to get hold of this decretal, and he wrote urgently to the Pope asking that it should be delivered into the king's hands, and shown to the Privy Council. "Without the Pope's compliance," he sadly wrote, "I cannot bear up against this storm." But Clement VII. felt that he was more dependent on Charles V. than on Henry VIII., and declared that he had granted the decretal merely to be shown to the king and then burned; he had never consented that it be shown to the king's counsellors. When he was further pressed he tossed his arms and said, with great agitation, "I do consider the ruin that hangs over me; I repent what I have done. If heresies arise, is it my fault? My conscience acquits me. None of you have any reason to complain. I have performed my promise, and the king and the cardinal have never asked anything in my power which I have not granted with the utmost readiness; but I will do no violence to my conscience. Let them, if they like, send the legate back again, on the pretext that he will not proceed in the cause, and then do as they please, provided they do not make me responsible for injustice."

Here the Pope touched upon a noticeable feature of

the case. Henry was bound upon a course which
was neither legally nor morally right, though national
interests might to some degree be pleaded in its behalf.
He was, however, resolved to be legally and morally
justified in his own eyes and in the eyes of others. He
would not content himself with setting aside the law,
and leaving it to others to prove him in the wrong. The
Papal Court was slow to justify him; it would have
been slower to condemn him. Most men would have
been satisfied with this knowledge, and would have
acted upon it. But Henry was not only minded to do
what he wished, but was resolved that what he wished
should be declared absolutely right. He was determined
that there should be no doubt about the legitimacy of
his children by Anne Boleyn ; and some recognition is
due to him for not allowing his desires to overcome his
patriotism, and leave to England the deplorable legacy
of a disputed succession. As a man, Henry did not
strive to subject his desires to the law of right; as a
king, he was bent upon justifying his own caprice so
that it should not do hurt to his royal office, or offend
his duty to his kingdom. Henry sinned, but he was
bent on sinning royally, and believed that so he could
extenuate his sin.

Not only was Campeggio ordered not to part with
the decretal, but he was bidden to destroy it. Meanwhile a new feature of the case emerged. It became
known that, besides the bull of dispensation granted to
Henry VII., an ampler brief had been issued in confirmation of it to Ferdinand of Spain, of which the
original was contained in the Spanish archives. Henry
VIII. insisted on its production, in the hopes of destroy

ing it or casting doubts on its authenticity, and new negotiations were begun about this brief, which had the effect of wasting time and deferring the trial of the case. Further, on Clement VII.'s return to Rome in May he was attacked by illness, and his death was reported. Nothing could be done by the legates till they were assured of his recovery.

Meanwhile Henry was growing more and more impatient, and made it clear to Wolsey that if the proceedings did not lead to his divorce all the blame would be laid at Wolsey's door. Anne Boleyn also began to suspect Wolsey's good intentions towards herself, and thought that he was responsible for these repeated delays. Wolsey could no longer doubt that his all was staked on the issue of the trial, which at length began at Blackfriars on 18th June 1529. Katharine appeared, and protested against the jurisdiction of the court. For the purpose of deciding this point it was necessary that both parties should appear in person; and on 21st June Henry and Katharine both were present. The king demanded instant judgment for the easing of his conscience; Katharine first knelt before the king and asked for pity, then she appealed to Rome, where only the cause could be decided without partiality or suspicion. The legates overruled her appeal, and on her non-appearance declared her contumacious.

The summoning of the king and queen was merely a formal incident in the procedure of the court, but it strangely impressed itself upon men's minds. The king, whom they regarded as the fountain of law, was called to plead before one of his own subjects and a foreign priest. Apart from any thought of the question at issue, or its rights and wrongs, Englishmen marvelled at this indignity, and felt that ecclesiastical law was some foreign thing which they could not fathom. No doubt the impression then wrought upon their minds accounts in some measure for the acceptance of the royal supremacy, as being at least more intelligible than the actual working of the outworn theory of the supremacy of the Pope.

Moreover, the suppliant attitude of Katharine awakened a strong feeling of compassion, which on 28th June found expression from the upright Bishop of Rochester, John Fisher, who appeared to plead Katharine's cause, and declared himself ready to follow the example of John the Baptist and lay down his life, if need be, to maintain the sanctity of matrimony. Others followed his example, and the signs of some dislike to the king's proceedings amongst Englishmen encouraged Campeggio to fall back upon his policy of procrastination, which the impetuous zeal of Wolsey was striving to overcome.

Henry grew more and more angry at the signs of opposition to his will which met him on every side, and Wolsey had to bear the brunt of the royal wrath. Cavendish tells how one day Wolsey left the king's presence and took his barge. The Bishop of Carlisle, who was with him, remarked that the day was hot. "Yea," quoth my lord cardinal, "if ye had been as well chafed as I have been within this hour ye would say it was very hot." He went home "to his naked bed," where in two hours' time he was found by Lord Wiltshire, who brought a message from the king, bidding him and Campeggio "repair unto the queen at Bridewell, into her chamber, to persuade her by their wisdoms, advising her to surrender the whole matter unto the king's hands by her own will and consent, which should be much better to her honour than to stand to the trial of law and be condemned, which would seem much to her slander and defamation." Wolsey vainly complained of the folly of the lords of the Council in putting such fancies into the king's head : he was bound to rise and obey. Sadly he sought Campeggio, and with a sense of deep humiliation the two judges set out to make another attempt to browbeat an accused who had already refused to submit to their judicial authority.

On 23d July it was expected that the court would give its decision. The king was present in a gallery, and after the reading of the pleas his counsel demanded judgment. Campeggio rose and declared that as the vacation of the Roman courts began at the end of July and lasted till October, he must follow that custom, and adjourn the sittings of the court for two months. On this the Duke of Suffolk slapped the table and exclaimed, "It was never merry in England whilst we had cardinals among us." Wolsey was not the man to brook an insult, especially from one whom he had greatly benefited. "Sir," he said, "of all men within this realm ye have least cause to dispraise or be offended at cardinals: for if I, a simple cardinal, had not been, you should have had at this present no head upon your shoulders, wherein you should have a tongue to make any such report of us, who intend you no manner of displeasure."

But though Wolsey could still wear a bold face when attacked, he knew that the future was hopeless. His enemies were daily gaining ground. His place, as the king's trusted counsellor, was taken by Stephen Gardiner, whom he had trained, and who was now the king's secretary and Anne Boleyn's chief agent. The old nobles, headed by the Duke of Norfolk, had made common cause with the relations of Anne Boleyn, and saw their opportunity of avenging themselves for all the slights which Wolsey had put upon them. Henry was unwilling to abandon all hopes of his divorce through the legatine court, and spared Wolsey for a time; but Wolsey knew that the ground was slipping from under him. The Pope resolved to revoke the cause to Rome, and recall the powers granted to the legates; it required all Wolsey's efforts to prevent the issue of a citation to Henry to appear before the Roman court.

Moreover, Wolsey had the additional pang of seeing all the fruits of his diplomatic activity abandoned before the absorbing interest of this miserable matter of the king's domestic life. If there was one object which was dear to Wolsey's heart, it was to secure England's power in Europe by a close alliance with France. For this purpose he had made great sacrifices, and he thought that he had some claim on Francis I.'s gratitude. Yet Francis was negotiating for peace with Charles V., and a conference was being held at Cambrai between his mother Louise and .Charles's aunt Margaret. Wolsey sorely longed to be present at that conference and protect the interests of England; but Henry VIII had no interest in such matters, and only regarded Wolsey's wish as a sign that he was lukewarm in his efforts for the divorce. Moreover, Francis I. defamed him to the English envoy, the Duke of Suffolk, and did his best to foster the king's suspicion of Wolsey's zeal in "the great matter." He knew that to deprive Henry of his

N

acute adviser was the readiest means of hiding his own
proceedings. The conference at Cambrai was an abandonment of the methods of diplomacy and a return to
the old usages of the days of chivalry. Two women
took counsel together about family affairs, and their
object was to remove domestic difficulties. Really
Francis I. was weary of a profitless warfare, and agreed
to abandon Italy to Charles V. Henry VIII. was ap-
peased by a transference of the debt of Charles V. to
the shoulders of Francis I., and this promise of more
money seems to have satisfied the English king. Early
in August the peace was signed, and Henry was included in its provisions. If a testimony were needed
that entirely English diplomacy depended upon Wolsey,
it would be found in Henry's short-sightedness at
this time. He did not try to influence the proceedings at Cambrai, but allowed himself to be hoodwinked
by Francis I., even in the point about which he was
most interested. The peace of Cambrai left Charles V.
supreme in Italy, and restored in name the authority of
the Pope, which the two sovereigns declared themselves
resolved to maintain. Its practical result was to make
the Pope more anxious to please Charles, who was
now most closely connected with his political interests,
and to free him from the dread of an alliance between
Henry and Francis, which might have brought pressure
to bear upon his action in the divorce. Clement
had now no special motive for trying to conciliate the
English king, and it was clear to all Europe that Wolsey
no longer guided England's policy.

It was not only that Wolsey had failed in the matter
of the divorce, but his failure had brought to light the

true nature of the policy which he was pursuing, and
had shown that it was not adapted to the turn which
affairs were taking under the influence of the king's
personal desires.   Wolsey had planned a conservative
reform, to be carried out gradually.   England, respected
on the Continent, and holding the balance between
France and the Empire, was gradually to assert its
power and independence by setting up a strong monarchy which should overawe the Papacy, and without
any formal breach with past traditions, should remodel
its ecclesiastical institutions, and put its relations to the
Papacy on a new footing.   Henry VIII. had so far
entered into the spirit of this plan as to regard the
existing state of things as of little moment, and his
wishes led him to try and anticipate the future.   This
was the most disastrous thing that could have befallen
Wolsey : it is the danger which besets all attempts at
conservative reform.   It is hard to train men in the
ideas of future change, and expect them to submit
patiently to present fetters.   Henry brusquely demanded too much from the Pope, and the Pope in his
alarm offered too little.   Wolsey tried to mediate, but
he was too closely allied with Henry for the Pope to
trust him, and when his object was clearly seen in a
small matter he was deprived of the means by which he
hoped to win.   His method was framed for large operations on a large field ; it was not suited for the petty
task which was suddenly imposed upon him.   Yet if it
failed there it was sure to be condemned altogether, and
the future would belong to the more revolutionary forces
which he had been trying to hold in check

So in proportion as Wolsey failed about the divorce,

the threads of his different but converging schemes fell
from his hands. What was the profit to Henry of
Wolsey's intricate foreign policy if it did not allow him
to get a divorce when he pleased? Why should he
deal tenderly with the papal authority when it threw
such obstacles in his way? Why should he spare the
Church when its bishops protested against him? Why
should he permit the slow transformation of the monasteries when with a little trouble their spoil would fall
into his hands? Why should he trust to Wolsey, who
had already failed him in his need, when he had men
like Gardiner, with clear heads about matters of details,
to serve him at his need? Above all, why should
Wolsey's fine-drawn plans stand between him and his
people's affections, and lead him to do what Englishmen
neither understood nor approved? These were the
questions with which Henry was plied. Wolsey had
been only too successful and too consistent. If his
policy was abandoned in aught, it must be abandoned
in all. When Henry let fall Wolsey's foreign policy,
and made no effort to influence the peace of Cambrai,
there was no further need of Wolsey in England's
councils, and his rule was practically at an end.

Still Wolsey was permitted to retain his offices.
Campeggio had not yet departed; something might
still be done. The king had for some time avoided
seeing Wolsey, and was engaged in wandering from
place to place in the company of Anne Boleyn. At
last, in the middle of September, Campeggio prepared
to return to Rome, and accompanied by Wolsey went
to take leave of the king, who was then at Grafton in
Northamptonshire. There they arrived on 19th Septem-

ber, and Campeggio was shown to his room, but Wolsey
was informed that there was no room provided for him.
He was relieved from his astonishment by a groom of
the stole, who said, "I assure you, sir, here is very
little room in this house, scantly sufficient for the king.
However, I beseech your grace to accept mine for a
season." When Wolsey and Campeggio were ushered
into the king's presence they found the lords of the
Council eagerly watching the king's behaviour. If they
expected any signs of the royal displeasure they were
disappointed, as Henry received Wolsey most graciously,
and drew him aside into a window, where he talked
with him privately.

The king dined privately with Anne Boleyn, and
Wolsey dined with the lords of the Council. In course
of conversation he hinted at his own intentions for the
future by saying, "It were well done if the king
would send his chaplains and bishops to their cures and
benefices." The Duke of Norfolk eagerly assented, and
Wolsey went on to say that he would gladly go to his
bishopric of Winchester. Then Norfolk showed his
fears by saying, "Nay, to your see of York, whence
comes both your greatest honour and charge." Already
Wolsey's foes were scheming to remove him as far as
possible from the royal presence.

Every one was eagerly watching and listening for the
smallest indications of the royal pleasure; and Cavendish was told that Anne Boleyn at dinner with the
king showed her dissatisfaction at Wolsey's kindly reception. She denounced the cardinal in no measured
terms, but without any immediate result, as after dinner
the king called Wolsey into his private room and talked

with him for some time; "the which blanked his
enemies very sore, and made them to stir the coals,
being in doubt what this matter would grow into,
having now none other refuge to trust to but Mistress
Anne, in whom was all their whole and firm trust and
affiance." Wolsey rode off to "Master Empson's house,
called Euston, three miles from Grafton," where he
spent the night, and received a visit from Gardiner,
who was thought to come as a spy; but Wolsey talked
to him about indifferent subjects, and showed that his
sense of personal dignity was still strong.

Next morning he rode early to the Court, and saw
the king for a short time; but Anne Boleyn had prepared
a picnic at Hatwell Park, and carried off Henry with
her, that Wolsey might not have much opportunity for
private talk. The king bade a hurried farewell to
Wolsey and Campeggio, and then rode away with Anne,
while the legates returned to London. Campeggio did
not reach Dover till 8th October, and before he was
allowed to embark his luggage was ransacked by the
king's officials.

This extraordinary violation of the privileges of an
ambassador was characteristic of the unscrupulous meanness to which Henry was now ready to descend. He
hoped to find amongst Campeggio's papers the Pope's
decretal about the law of the divorce. If he had found
it Wolsey might still have been useful. He might have
been compelled to continue the proceedings of the
legatine court, and give judgment in Henry's favour,
sheltering himself under the terms of the commission,
and applying the interpretation of the decretal. In this
way the first measures wrung out of the Pope when he

wished to be conciliating might have been used in a
high-handed fashion against the conclusions of his settled
policy.   But Campeggio had already been instructed by
the Pope to burn the decretal.   Nothing was found as
the result of the search, which only revealed the cardinal's
poverty.   He had come to England ill provided, and had
gained nothing from the royal bounty.

This unworthy device seems to have been of Henry's
own devising; and as soon as he heard of its failure
Wolsey's doom was sealed.   The king had treated him
graciously, to the dismay even of Anne Boleyn, a few
days before; now he abandoned him to his enemies,
who had their weapons of attack in readiness.   On 9th
October the king's attorney sued for a writ of *præmunire*
against Wolsey, on the ground that his acts done as
legate were contrary to the statute.   After this Wolsey's
ruin was a foregone conclusion.

CHAPTER X

THE FALL OF WOLSEY

1529–1530

WHEN the storm broke over his head Wolsey had no hope of escape. His position as an English minister was due entirely to the king's favour, and when that favour was withdrawn he was entirely helpless. Outside the king there was no motive power in English politics at this period. There was no party in the State strong enough to bring any influence to bear upon him : he was likely to be moved by nothing save the dread of a popular rising, and there was no chance of a popular rising in Wolsey's favour. On the other hand, Wolsey had been contented to take upon his own shoulders the responsibility of all that was most unpopular in the king's proceedings. The demands created by the king's extravagance were put down to his extortionate nature ; the debts incurred by a policy which he disapproved were supposed to be the results of his influence ; even the divorce was attributed to his ill-will against the Emperor and his love for France. The current of popular opinion ran strong against Wolsey. He had made few friends and many enemies. His enemies were powerful, his friends were powerless. No one in England could lend him any help.

It is true that the charge brought against him was most iniquitous. He had obtained his legatine authority through the king's urgent request; he had used it solely at the king's orders, and in the king's behalf. But he knew that such a plea would not be regarded, as the king's courts would simply register the king's will. There was no other course than entire submission, and before the king Wolsey had no thought of personal dignity. He wrote to Henry as a lowly suppliant, "For surely, most gracious king, the remembrance of my folly, with the sharp sword of your Highness's displeasure, hath so penetrated my heart that I cannot but lamentably cry, It is enough; now stay, most merciful king, your hand." Such loyalty, such entire submission, is to our minds inconceivable, and only shows how the possession of absolute power debases not only those who are invested with it but those who are brought in contact with them. Wolsey might indeed lament his "folly" in putting any trust in princes; he had served his master only too well, and met with the basest ingratitude for all the sacrifices of his own wishes and his own principles.

Still he hoped by his submission to save something. If sentence were pronounced against him, under the charge of *præmunire*, his goods would be forfeited, and his acts invalidated. If he threw himself upon the king's mercy he might at least save his two colleges, and might be permitted to serve his country on a smaller scale. What was coming he could not foresee. There would be open war between Henry and the Papacy, waged with

new weapons and fraught with danger to the English
Church. "It is the intention of these lords," wrote the
French ambassador, "when Wolsey is dead or destroyed,
to get rid of the Church and spoil the goods of both.
I suppose they mean to do grand things." The days of
revolution were at hand, and Wolsey might still have
some power to check its excesses.

His submission led to no immediate results. On 16th
October the Dukes of Norfolk and Suffolk demanded the
surrender of the great seal, and ordered Wolsey to depart
to his house at Esher. Wolsey would humble himself
before the king, but not before others, and calmly asked
them for their authority. They answered that they had
the king's commission by word of mouth. "The great
seal of England," said Wolsey, "was delivered me by
the king's own person, to enjoy during my life, with the
ministration of the office and high room of chancellorship of England; for my surety whereof I have the
king's letters-patent to show." High words were used
by the dukes, but in the end they departed, and reap-
peared next day with letters from the king. On reading
them Wolsey delivered up the seal, and expressed himself content to withdraw to Esher.

Before departing he made an inventory of all his
plate and tapestries, that it might be ready for the
king to take possession. He further signed an indenture
acknowledging that on the authority of bulls obtained
from Rome, which he published in England contrary to
the statute, he had unlawfully vexed the prelates of the
realm and other of the king's subjects, thereby incurring
the penalties of *præmunire*, by which also he deserved to
suffer perpetual imprisonment at the king's pleasure, and

to forfeit all his lands, offices, and goods.   He besought
the king, in part recompense of his offences, to take into
his hands all his temporal possessions.   Then he entered
his barge in the presence of a crowd, which was sorely
disappointed not to see him take the way to the Tower.

When Wolsey arrived at Putney he was greeted by a
messenger from the king, who brought him as a token a
ring, with a message "that the king bade him be of good
cheer, for he should not lack.   Although the king hath
dealt with you unkindly, he saith that it is for no displeasure that he beareth you, but only to satisfy the
minds of some which he knoweth be not your friends.
Also ye know right well that he is able to recompense
you with twice as much as your goods amounteth unto :
and all this he bade me that I should show you.   Therefore, sir, take patience ; and for my part, I trust to see
you in better estate than ever ye were."   When Wolsey
heard this he dismounted from his mule and knelt in the
mud in sign of thankfulness.   He gave a present to the
messenger, and grieved that he had no worthy gift to
send to the king.   Presently he bethought himself of
a jester belonging to his household.   "If ye would at
my request present the king with this poor fool, I trust
his Highness would accept him well, for surely for a
nobleman's pleasure he is worth a thousand pounds."
It is a relief to find in this dismal story some signs of
human feeling. ˙ "The poor fool took on so, and fired so
in such a rage when he saw that he must needs depart
from my lord," that six tall yeomen had to be sent as an
escort to convey him safely to the Court.

It is needless to seek for a motive for Henry's conduct
in sending this delusive message ; probably he did it

through an amiable desire to make himself generally
agreeable. No man likes to feel that he is acting vil-
lainously; perhaps Henry's conscience felt all the pleasure
of having performed a virtuous action when he heard of
Wolsey's gratitude for such a small mercy. Henry VIII.
was nothing if he was not conscientious; but he made
large drafts on his conscience, and paid them back in
small coin. Probably we have here the record of such a
payment.

Certainly Henry did nothing to give his goodwill towards Wolsey any practical expression; he did
not even send him any money to provide his household
with the necessaries of life. For a month they remained
"without beds, sheets, tablecloths, cups, and dishes to
eat their meat or lie in," and ultimately had to borrow
them. What most distressed Wolsey, who had been
accustomed to munificence, was that he had not even
money to pay the wages of his household before he dis-
missed them sadly from his service. In his straits one
of his officials came to his aid, and showed his tact and
management in affairs of business. Thomas Cromwell,
the son of a London citizen, spent an adventurous youth
in business on the Continent, and settled in London as
a small attorney and a money-lender. Wolsey had
found out his ability, and employed him to manage the
dissolution of the monasteries, and transact the business
connected with the foundation of his colleges. No doubt
this gave him opportunities of spreading his own business, and making himself useful friends. In anticipa-
tion of the future he contrived to get himself elected as
member of the Parliament for which Henry VIII. issued
writs upon the suspension of the legatine court.

Cromwell accompanied Wolsey to Esher, and was much moved by the thought of the loss which his patron's fall was likely to inflict upon himself.   On 1st November Cavendish found him leaning in the window "with a primer in his hand, saying our Lady mattins.   He prayed not more earnestly than the tears distilled from his eyes."   He lamented that he was in disdain with most men for his master's sake, and surely without just cause; but he was resolved that afternoon to ride to London, and so to the Court, "where I will either make or mar, or I come again."   After dinner he talked with Wolsey about his household, and then showed his power of gaining popularity at the expense of others.   "Have you not," he exclaimed, "a number of chaplains, to whom ye have departed very liberally with spiritual promotions? and yet have your poor servants taken much more pains for you in one day than all your idle chaplains have done in a year.   Therefore if they will not freely and frankly consider your liberality, and depart with you of the same goods gotten in your service, now in your great indigence and necessity, it is pity that they live."   Wolsey agreed; he summoned his household, and addressed them in a dignified speech; he gave them a month's holiday, that they might seek some more profitable service.   Then Cromwell said that they lacked money, and himself tendered five pounds towards their payment, adding, "Now let us see what your chaplains will do."   The example was contagious, and contributions poured in.   The household was paid, and departed full of thankfulness to Cromwell.   Then, after a private conversation with Wolsey, Cromwell rode off to London to "make or mar."

Parliament met on 3d November, and Wolsey's enemies hoped that its first business would be Wolsey's impeachment. For this, however, Henry VIII. was not prepared, though he did not openly forbid it. He was not sure of the capacity of his new advisers, and perhaps felt that he might have further need of Wolsey's services. Anyhow it was better to keep his opponents in constant fear of his return to power. They were bound together rather by opposition to Wolsey than by any agreement amongst themselves; and Henry was not very sanguine about their administrative success. The Duke of Norfolk, the uncle of Anne Boleyn, was president of the Council, and Suffolk was vice-president. The chancellorship was given to Sir Thomas More, who was well fitted by his literary reputation and high character to calm the fears of moderate men, and show Europe that the English king had no lack of eminent servants. The chancellorship of the duchy of Lancashire was given to the treasurer of the household, Sir William Fitzwilliam, a capable official. Gardiner preferred an ecclesiastical post, and succeeded to the bishopric of Winchester, which Wolsey was bidden to resign. It still remained to be seen if Norfolk, Suffolk, and More could fill the place of Wolsey.

Parliament was opened by the king; and the chancellor, according to custom, made a speech. In the course of it More showed that a man of letters does not necessarily retain his literary taste in politics, and that high character does not save a statesman from the temptation to catch a passing cheer by unworthy taunts at his defeated adversary. He spoke of the king as shepherd of his people, and went on, " As you see that amongst a great flock of sheep some be rotten and faulty, which the good shepherd sendeth from the good sheep, so the great wether which is of late fallen, as you all know, so craftily, ·so scabbedly, yea, and so untruly juggled with the king, that all men must needs guess and think that he thought in himself that he had no wit to perceive his crafty doing, or else that he presumed that the king would not see nor know his fraudulent juggling and attempts. But he was deceived; for his Grace's sight was so quick and penetrating that he saw him, yea, and saw through him, both within and without, so that all things to him were open; and according to his deserts he hath had a gentle correction."

This speech of More served as introductory to a Bill which was brought into the Upper House for disabling Wolsey from being restored to his former dignities and place in the king's Council. It was founded upon a series of articles which had been drawn up by his enemies long before, and were a tissue of frivolous or groundless charges. The Bill passed the Lords, but on its introduction into the Commons was opposed by Cromwell, who knew that the king did not wish it to be passed. It answered its purpose of casting a stigma on Wolsey, and justifying Henry's conduct towards him; but Henry did not intend to deprive himself of the power of employing Wolsey again if he should prove useful. So Cromwell served the king while he served Wolsey, and served himself at the same time by a display of zeal for his fallen master which raised him in men's esteem, "so that at length, for his honest behaviour in his master's cause, he grew into such estimation in every man's opinion, that he was esteemed to be the

most faithfullest servant to his master of all others,
wherein he was of all men greatly commended." Moreover, he managed to make friends by the sure tie of
self-interest. He advised Wolsey to buy off the hostility
of important men by granting them pensions out of
the revenues of his see : as he chose the recipients of
the money and negotiated the grants he gained more
gratitude than Wolsey gained profit out of the trans-
action. Wolsey believed that his prospects depended
on Cromwell's zeal, and the great cardinal became submissive to the direction of one whom he had raised.
He abode at Esher in a state of feverish anxiety, sometimes receiving a present and a gracious message from
the king, often irritated by Cromwell, who deluded him
by a cheap display of zeal, grieving most of all at the
uncertainty of the fortunes of his great colleges, which
he still wished to leave as a memorial to posterity of the
schemes which he intended.

Parliament was prorogued in the middle of December,
and the Bill against Wolsey was allowed to drop. The
king and Anne Boleyn were delighted with the cardinal's
house at York Place, of which they took possession,
and Wolsey was still left in uncertainty about his future.
Anxiety preyed upon his health, and at Christmas he fell
ill. The news of his illness seems to have brought some
remorse to Henry, who sent his own physician, and eagerly
asked for tidings, saying, "I would not lose him for
twenty thousand pounds." Doctor Buttes answered,
"Then must your Grace send him some comfortable
message as shortly as is possible." The king gave Buttes
a favourite ring from his own finger, saying, "Tell him
that I am not offended with him in my heart nothing at

all, and that shall he perceive, and God send him life very shortly." He asked Anne Boleyn to send also a "token with comfortable words," and Anne at his command obeyed, overcoming her reluctance by the thought that the cardinal was on his deathbed.

Doctor Buttes's prescription was a good one, and with revived hopes Wolsey speedily recovered. On 2d February 1530 the king sent him some furniture for his house and chapel. On 12th February he received a full pardon for his offences, and on 14th February was restored to the archbishopric of York and its possessions excepting York Place, which the king retained for himself. He entreated to be allowed to keep also the bishopric of Winchester and the Abbey of St. Alban's; but Gardiner had his eye on Winchester, and the Dukes of Norfolk and Suffolk were anxious that Wolsey should not hold a post which might bring him into the neighbourhood of the king. He was compelled to resign both these offices, and recognised in this the power of his foes

The damp air of Esher was hurtful to his health, and he received permission to change his residence to Richmond Lodge. There he stayed until the state of the roads allowed him to take his journey northwards, which the Duke of Norfolk pressed him to do in forcible language. "Show him," he said to Cromwell, "that if he go not away shortly, I will, rather than he should tarry still, tear him with my teeth." When Wolsey heard this he said, "Marry, Thomas, then it is time to be going, if my lord of Norfolk take it so. Therefore I pray you go to the king and say that I would with all my heart go to my benefice at York but for want of money." Wolsey's immediate necessities were grudgingly supplied by the lords of the Council, and in the beginning of Passion Week he began his journey to York. He was received with courtesy by the gentry on the way. The manor-house at Southwell, where he resolved to live, required some repairs, and he could not occupy it till 5th June.

In his house at Southwell Wolsey received the neighbouring gentry, and made himself popular amongst them. He lived simply, and applied himself to the discharge of the duties of his office with great success. A pamphlet published in 1536 says of him : " Who was less beloved in the north than my lord cardinal before he was amongst them ? Who better beloved after he had been there a while ? He gave bishops a right good example how they might win men's hearts. There were few holy days but he would ride five or six miles from his house, now to this parish church, now to that, and there cause one or other of his doctors to make a sermon unto the people. He sat amongst them and said mass before all the parish ; he saw why churches were made ; he began to restore them to their right and proper use ; he brought his dinner with him, and bade divers of the parish to it. He inquired whether there were any debate or grudge between any of them. If there were, after dinner he sent for the parties to the church and made them all one." It is an attractive picture of episcopal activity which is here set before us. We wish that Wolsey had been great enough to realise the pleasure of these simple duties so thoroughly as to wean himself from the allurements of political ambition. But Wolsey in his retirement was something like Machiavelli in exile : he found some satisfaction for his activity in the doings of peasants, but he went home and hankered for the great life of politics which was denied him. He meditated still how he could overthrow his enemies and return to the more complex problems in which he had been trained.

At the end of the summer Wolsey removed from Southwell to another manor-house at Scrooby, where he continued the same mode of life. All this time his actions were jealously watched by his enemies, who suspected him of trying to gain popularity and raise up a party in his favour. They did their best to keep him in perpetual annoyance by threats of legal proceedings touching the possessions of the see of York. The king paid no heed to him save to exact all the money he could from his forfeiture. Amongst other things which the king claimed was the payment of Wolsey's pension from the French king; and his care for Wolsey's health at Christmas may have been due to the fact that he thought that Wolsey's life had a pecuniary value to himself. He presently dissolved Wolsey's college at Ipswich, and seized all its lands and possessions. It was a bitter blow to Wolsey to see his plans thus overthrown. He had hoped to found an institution which should promote education where it was sorely needed in the eastern counties. It was the beginning of a project which would have led to the foundation of local universities, which it has been reserved to our own day to revive. If Wolsey had remained in power monastic revenues would have been increasingly diverted to educational purposes, and England would have been provided with colleges which would have grown with local needs. The dissolution of the college at Ipswich checked this process at the begin-

ning, and negatived any scheme for the slow transformation of the monasteries into institutions which were in
accordance with national needs.

Cardinal College at Oxford met with better fortune.
Wolsey pleaded hard for its preservation, and the authori-
ties of the college made a stand in its behalf.   The king
was not yet prepared to seize the lands of the dissolved
monastery of St. Frideswyde, or of the old Canterbury
Hall, which had been absorbed, and it could be shown
that he would lose as much as he would gain by attempt-
ing an accurate division of the property of the college.
He agreed to "have an honourable college there, but not
so great and of such magnificence as my lord cardinal
intended to have, for it is not thought meet for the
common weal of our realm."   The site of the college
and a portion of its revenues were saved from the commissioners who were realising Wolsey's forfeiture; but
the name of Christ Church obliterated that of Cardinal
College, and Henry VIII. endeavoured as far as he could
to associate the foundation with himself and dissociate it
from Wolsey.

This persistent disregard of the ideas which Wolsey
had striven to put forward weighed heavily on his
spirits.   "I am put from my sleep and meat," he wrote,
"for such advertisements as I have had of the dissolution of my colleges."   It was not only the sense of
personal disappointment which afflicted him; it was the
hopeless feeling that all his policy was being reversed.
Wolsey was in his way a churchman, and hoped as a
statesman to bring the Church into accordance with the
national needs.   He saw that only in this way could the
existing resources of the Church be saved from the hand

of the spoiler. The king's desire to seize upon the
revenues of his colleges showed him that Henry had
cast away the principles which Wolsey had striven to
enforce, that he had broken through the limits which
Wolsey had endeavoured to set, and that when once
he had tasted his prey his appetite was likely to be in-
satiable. This taught Wolsey that his own future was
hopeless. On the lower level to which the king had
sunk he was not likely to need the cardinal's aid.
Wolsey's great schemes for the future were to make way
for a policy mainly dictated by present greed. Henry
VIII. had discovered how great his power was, and
intended to use it for the satisfaction of his own desires.

So Wolsey turned himself more attentively to the
duties of his episcopal office, hoping thereby to make
some amends for past neglect, and fill up with useful
work the remainder of his days His poverty had prevented him from taking possession of his cathedral, as
he had no money to defray the expenses of his installation. By the end of September he had managed to
scrape together £1500, and set out from Scrooby to
York. On his way he was busied with confirmations.
At St. Oswald's Abbey he confirmed children from eight
in the morning till noon ; after dinner he returned to
the church at one, and continued his confirmation till
four, when he was constrained for weariness to sit down
in a chair. Next morning before his departure he confirmed a hundred children more ; and as he rode on his
way he found at Ferrybridge two hundred children waiting for confirmation at a stone cross standing upon the
green. It was late in the evening before he reached
Cawood Castle, seven miles from York. There he was

visited by the Dean of York, and made arrangements for his installation.

This ceremony, however, was not to take place. Wolsey's enemies were implacable, especially the Duke of Norfolk, who was alarmed at the renewal of Wolsey's popularity in the north, and at the signs of vigour which he showed. His actions were jealously watched and eagerly criticised to find some opportunity for a charge against him, which was at last found in Wolsey's communications with foreign envoys. It would seem that Wolsey could not reconcile himself to political inactivity, and trusted that the influence of Francis I., for whom he had done so much, would be used in his favour. But Francis treated Wolsey with the proverbial ingratitude of politicians. Wolsey had been a friend of France, but his friendship had been costly, and Francis I. found that the new ministers were equally friendly to France, and did not demand so much in return. In truth, Henry, though he had abandoned Wolsey for his failure in the matter of the divorce, had not been better served by his new advisers, who had no other course to follow than that which Wolsey had marked out—to use the close alliance with France as a means of bringing pressure to bear upon the Pope. So Norfolk was obsequious to Francis, who preferred to deal with a man of Norfolk's calibre rather than acknowledge a master in Wolsey.

Of this Wolsey was ignorant; and he no longer showed his old dexterity in promoting his own interests. He made the mistake of trusting to the old methods of diplomacy when his position was no longer that of a minister, and when he had been removed from actual touch of current affairs. He opened up communications with the French envoy by means of a Venetian physician, Agostino, who was a member of his household. He even communicated with the imperial envoy as well. However harmless these communications might be, they were certainly indiscreet, and were capable of being represented to the king as dangerous. Norfolk gained some information, either from the French envoy or from Agostino, and laid before the king charges against Wolsey, "that he had written to Rome to be reinstated in his possessions, and to France for its favour; and was returning to his ancient pomp, and corrupting the people." There was not much in these charges; but Norfolk was afraid of Wolsey in the background, and quailed before the king's bursts of petulance, in which he said that the cardinal knew more about the business of the State than any of his new advisers. Henry was quite satisfied with the proceeds of spoiling Wolsey, and was glad to keep him in reserve; but the suggestion that Wolsey was intriguing with foreign Courts sorely angered him, and he gave orders that Wolsey be brought to trial to answer for his conduct.

So Sir Walter Walshe was sent with a warrant to the Earl of Northumberland, and arrived as Wolsey was busied at Cawood with the preliminaries of his installation. On 4th November, when Wolsey had retired from dinner and was sitting in his own room over his dessert, the Earl of Northumberland appeared, and demanded the keys of the castle from the porter. He entered the hall, and posted his servants to guard all the doors. Wolsey, in ignorance of what was in store for him, met Northumberland and offered him hospitality, expressing his delight at the unexpected visit. When they were alone the Earl, "trembling, said, with a very faint and soft voice, unto my lord, laying his hand upon his arm, 'My lord, I arrest you of high treason.'" For a time Wolsey stood speechless with astonishment, then he asked to see the warrant, which Northumberland had not brought with him. As he was speaking Sir Walter Walshe opened the door and thrust into the room the physician Agostino, whom he had made prisoner. Wolsey asked him about the warrant, and when he recognised him as one of the gentlemen of the king's privy chamber, he submitted to the royal commands without asking further for the production of the warrant. Then he delivered up his keys to Northumberland.

Agostino was at once sent to London tied under a horse's belly—a mode of conveyance which was doubtless calculated to refresh his memory. When he arrived in London he was taken to the Duke of Norfolk's house, and showed himself ready to bear witness against Wolsey. "Since they have had the cardinal's physician in their hands," writes the imperial envoy, "they have found what they sought. Since he has been here he has lived in the Duke of Norfolk's house like a prince, and is singing the tune they wished."

There was not the same need of haste in bringing Wolsey to London, for even with Agostino's help Norfolk was doubtful if the evidence against Wolsey would be sufficient to ensure his condemnation to death; and he did not wish to give Wolsey the opportunity of a trial when he might still be formidable. His imprisonment in the Tower at the royal pleasure would only bring him nearer to the king, who might at any moment make use of him as he threatened. Really, Norfolk was somewhat embarrassed at the success of his scheme ; and Wolsey, in a conversation with Cavendish, showed a flash of his old greatness. "If I may come to my answer," he said, "I fear no man alive ; for he liveth not upon the earth that shall look upon this face and shall be able to accuse me of any untruth ; and that know my enemies full well, which will be an occasion that I shall not have indifferent justice, but they will rather seek some other sinister way to destroy me."

It was this thought that unnerved Wolsey, worn out as he was by disappointment, humiliated by his helplessness, and harassed by a sense of relentless persecution. Still he retained his dignity and kindliness, and when on the evening of 7th November he was told to prepare for his journey, he insisted upon bidding farewell to his household. The Earl of Northumberland wished to prevent this, and only gave way through fear of a tumult if he persisted in his refusal. The servants knelt weeping before Wolsey, who "gave them comfortable words and worthy praises for their diligent faithfulness and honest truth towards him, assuring them that what chance soever should happen unto him, that he was a true man and a just to his sovereign lord." Then shaking each of them by the hand he departed.

Outside the gate the country folk had assembled to the number of three thousand, who cried, "God save your grace. The foul evil take all them that hath thus taken you from us ; we pray God that a very vengeance may light upon them." Thus they ran crying after him through the town of Cawood, they loved him so well. After this moving farewell Wolsey rode through the gathering darkness to Pomfret, where he was lodged in the abbey. Thence he proceeded through Doncaster to Sheffield Park, where he was kindly received by the Earl of Shrewsbury, whose guest he was for eighteen days. Once a day the earl visited him and tried to comfort him, but Wolsey refused all human comfort, and applied himself diligently to prayer. While he was at Sheffield Park his health, which never had been good, began to give way, and he suffered from dysentery, which was aggravated by an unskilful apothecary.

As he was thus ailing there arrived Sir William Kingston, Constable of the Tower, with a guard of twenty-four soldiers; he had received a commission from the king to bring Wolsey as a prisoner to the Tower. It would seem from this that Agostino's confessions had been skilfully raised to fan the royal wrath, and Henry gave this sign that he was prepared to treat his former minister as a traitor. The Earl of Shrewsbury did his best to treat the coming of Kingston as a trivial incident, and sent Cavendish to break the news gently to his master. Cavendish gave the message as he was bidden. "Forsooth my lord of Shrewsbury, perceiving by your often communication that ye were always desirous to come before the king's Majesty, and now as your assured friend, hath travailed so with his letters unto the king, that the king hath sent for you by Master Kingston and twenty-four of the guard to conduct you to his Highness." Wolsey was not deceived. "Master Kingston," he repeated, and smote his thigh. When Cavendish made a further attempt to cheer him he cut him short by saying, "I perceive more than you can imagine or can know. Ex-

perience hath taught me." When Kingston was introduced and knelt before him, Wolsey said, " I pray you
stand up, and leave your kneeling unto a very wretch
replete with misery, not worthy to be esteemed, but for
a vile object utterly cast away, without desert ; and
therefore, good Master Kingston, stand up, or I will
myself kneel down by you." After some talk Wolsey
thanked Kingston for his kind words. " Assure yourself
that if I were as able and as lusty as I have been but of
late, I would not fail to ride with you in post. But all
these comfortable words which ye have spoken be but
for a purpose to bring me to a fool's paradise ; I know
what is provided for me."

With a mind thus agitated the sufferings of the
body increased. When Wolsey took his journey next day
all regarded him as a dying man. The soldiers of the
guard, " as soon as they espied their old master in such
a lamentable estate, lamented him with weeping eyes.
Whom my lord took by the hands, and divers times by
the way as he rode he would talk with them, sometime
with one and sometime with another." That night he
reached Hardwick Hall, in Notts, a house of the Earl of
Shrewsbury, and the next day rode to Nottingham. On
the way from thence to Leicester he was so feeble that
he could scarcely sit upon his mule. It was dark on
Saturday night when he reached Leicester Abbey, where
the abbot greeted him by torchlight. " Father Abbot,"
he said, " I am come hither to leave my bones among
you." Kingston had to carry him upstairs to his bed,
which he never quitted again.

All Sunday his malady increased, and on Monday
morning Cavendish, as he watched his face, thought

him drawing fast to his end. "He perceiving my shadow upon the wall by his bedside asked who was there. 'Sir, I am here,' quoth I. 'What is it of the clock?' said he. 'Forsooth, sir,' said I, 'it is past eight of the clock in the morning.'—'Eight of the clock, eight of the clock,' said he, rehearsing divers times. 'Nay, nay, it cannot be eight of the clock; for by eight of the clock ye shall lose your master, for my time draweth near that I must depart out of this world.'"

But the dying man was not to depart without a reminder of the pitiless character of the master whom he had served so well. When Wolsey left Cawood the Earl of Northumberland remained behind to examine his papers; amongst them he found a record that Wolsey had in his possession £1500, but he reported to the king that he could not find the money. Such was Henry's keenness as his own minister of finance that he could not await Wolsey's arrival in London, but wrote off instantly to Kingston, bidding him examine Wolsey how he came by the money, and discover where it was. In obedience to the royal command Kingston reluctantly visited the dying man, who told him that he had borrowed the money of divers friends and dependants whom he did not wish to see defrauded; the money was in the keeping of an honest man, and he asked for a little time before disclosing where it was.

In the night he often swooned, but rallied in the morning and asked for food. Some chicken broth was brought him, but he remembered that it was a fast-day, being St. Andrew's Eve. "What though it be," said his confessor, "ye be excused by reason of your sickness."—"Yea," said he, "what though? I will eat no

more." After this he made his confession, and abou
seven in the morning Kingston entered to ask further
about the money. But seeing how ill Wolsey was,
Kingston tried to comfort him. "Well, well," said
Wolsey, "I see the matter against me how it is framed,
but if I had served God so diligently as I have done
the king, he would not have given me over in my gray
hairs. Howbeit, this is the just reward that I must
receive for my worldly diligence and pains that I had
to do him service, only to satisfy his vain pleasure, not
regarding my godly duty. Wherefore, I pray you, with
all my heart, to have me most humbly commended unto
his royal Majesty, beseeching him in my behalf to call
to his most gracious remembrance all matters proceeding between him and me from the beginning of the
world unto this day, and the progress of the same, and
most chiefly in the weighty matter now depending (i.e.
the divorce); then shall his conscience declare whether
I have offended him or no. He is sure a prince of a
royal courage, and hath a princely heart; and rather
than he will either miss or want any part of his will or
appetite he will put the loss of one-half of his realm in
danger. For I assure you I have often kneeled before
him in his privy chamber on my knees the space of
an hour or two, to persuade him from his will and
appetite; but I could never bring to pass to dissuade
him therefrom. Therefore, Master Kingston, if it chance
hereafter you to be one of his Privy Council, as for
your wisdom and other qualities ye are meet to be,
I warn you to be well advised and assured what matter
ye put in his head, for ye shall never put it out again."
He went on to bid him warn the king against the spread of

the pernicious sect of Lutherans as harmful to the royal
authority and destructive of the order of the realm.
Then as his tongue failed him he gasped out, "Master
Kingston, farewell. I can no more, but wish all things
to have good success. My time draweth on fast. I may
not tarry with you. And forget not, I pray you, what
I have said and charged you withal, for when I am dead
ye shall peradventure remember my words much better."
His breath failed him and his eyes grew fixed. The
abbot came to administer supreme unction, and as the
clock struck eight Wolsey passed away. "And calling
to our remembrance his words the day before, how he
said that at eight of the clock we should lose our master,
one of us looked upon another supposing that he pro-
phesied of his departure."

Kingston sent a message to tell the king of Wolsey's
death, and hastened the preparations for his funeral.
His body was placed in a coffin of boards, vested in his
archiepiscopal robes, with his mitre, cross, and ring. It
lay in state till five in the afternoon, when it was carried
into the church and was placed in the Lady Chapel,
where it was watched all night. At four in the morning
mass was sung, and by six the grave had closed over
the remains of Wolsey.

It would be consoling to think that a pang of genuine
sorrow was felt by Henry VIII. when he heard of the
death of Wolsey; but unfortunately there is no ground
for thinking so, and all that is on record shows us that
Henry's chief care still was to get hold of the £1500,
which was all that remained of Wolsey's fortune.
Cavendish was taken by Kingston to Hampton Court,
where he was summoned to the king, who was engaged

in archery in the park. As Cavendish stood against
a tree sadly musing Henry suddenly came behind him
and slapped him on the back, saying, "I will make an
end of my game, and then I will talk with you." Soon
he finished his game and went into the garden, but kept
Cavendish waiting for some time outside. The interview
lasted more than an hour, "during which time he examined
me of divers matters concerning my lord, wishing that
liever than twenty thousand pounds that he had lived.
Then he asked me for the fifteen hundred pounds which
Master Kingston moved to my lord before his death."
Cavendish told him what he knew about it, and said
that it was deposited with a certain priest. "Well,
then," said the king, "let me alone, and keep this gear
secret between yourself and me, and let no man be privy
thereof; for if I hear more of it, then I know by whom
it is come to knowledge. Three may keep counsel if
two be away ; and if I thought that my cap knew my
counsel I would cast it into the fire and burn it."
Henry spoke freely, and these words disclose the secret
of his strength. Every politician has a method of his
own by which he hides his real character and assumes
a personality which is best fitted for his designs. Henry
VIII. beneath an air of frankness and geniality concealed a jealous and watchful temperament, full of crafty
designs for immediate gain, resolute, avaricious, and
profoundly self-seeking.

As we have been so much indebted to Cavendish
for an account of Wolsey's private life, especially in his
last days, it is worth while to follow Cavendish's fortunes.
The king promised to take him into his own service, and
to pay him his wages for the last year, amounting to

£10. He bade him ask it of the Duke of Norfolk. As he left the king he met Kingston coming from the Council, whither Cavendish also was summoned. Kingston implored him to take heed what he said. The Council would examine him about Wolsey's last words; "and if you tell them the truth you shall undo yourself." He had denied that he heard anything, and warned Cavendish to do the same. So Cavendish answered the Duke of Norfolk that he was so busied in waiting on Wolsey that he paid little heed to what he said. "He spoke many idle words, as men in such extremities do, the which I cannot now remember." He referred them to Kingston's more accurate memory. It is a dismal picture of Court life which is here presented to us. On every side was intrigue, suspicion, and deceit. Wolsey's last words were consigned to oblivion; for the frankness that was begotten of a retrospect in one who had nothing more to hope or fear was dangerous in a place whence truth was banished.

When the Council was over Norfolk talked with Cavendish about his future. Cavendish had seen enough of public life, and had no heart to face its dangers. The figure of Wolsey rose before his eyes, and he preferred to carry away into solitude his memories of the vanity of man's ambition. His only request was for a cart and horse to carry away his own goods, which had been brought with Wolsey's to the Tower. The king was gracious, and allowed him to choose six cart-horses and a cart from Wolsey's stable. He gave him five marks for his expenses, paid him £10 for arrears of wages, and added £20 as a reward. "I received all these things accordingly, and then I returned into my country."

It says much for Wolsey that he chose as his personal
attendant a man of the sweet, sensitive, retiring type of
George Cavendish, though it was not till after his fall
from power that he learned the value of such a friend.
No less significant of the times is the profound impression which Wolsey's fate excited on the mind of Cavendish, who in the retirement of his own county of Suffolk
lived with increasing sadness through the changes which
befell England and destroyed many of the memories
which were dearest to his heart. No one then cared to
hear about Wolsey, nor was it safe to recall the thought
of the great Cardinal of England to the minds of men
who were busied in undoing his work. Not till the days
of Mary did Cavendish gather together his notes and
sketch the fortunes of one whose figure loomed forth
from a distant past, mellowed by the mists of time, and
hallowed by the pious resignation which was the only
comfort that reflection could give to the helpless recluse.
The calm of a poetic sadness is expressed in the pages of
Cavendish's *Memoir*. Wolsey has become to him a type
of the vanity of human endeavour, and points the moral
of the superiority of a quiet life with God over the manifold activities of an aspiring ambition. But Cavendish
did not live to see the time when such a sermon, preached
on such a text, was likely to appeal to many hearers.
His work remained in manuscript, of which copies
circulated amongst a few. One such copy, it is clear,
must have reached the hands of Shakespeare, who, with
his usual quickness of perception, condensed as much as
his public could understand into his portrait of Wolsey
in the play of *Henry VIII*. When the *Memoir* was first
printed in 1641 it was garbled for party purposes. The

figure of Wolsey was long left to the portraiture of prejudice, and he was regarded only as the type of the arrogant ecclesiastic whom it was the great work of the Reformation to have rendered impossible in the future. Wolsey, the most patriotic of Englishmen, was branded as the minion of the Pope, and the upholder of a foreign despotism. When Fiddes, in 1724, attempted, on the strength of documents, to restore Wolsey to his due position amongst England's worthies, he was accused of Popery. Not till the mass of documents relating to the reign of Henry VIII. was published did it become possible for Dr. Brewer to show the significance of the schemes of the great cardinal, and to estimate his merits and his faults.

CHAPTER XI

THE WORK OF WOLSEY

"No statesman of such eminence ever died less lamented," is Dr. Brewer's remark on Wolsey's death. Indeed, the king had forgotten his old servant; his enemies rejoiced to be rid of a possible rival; the men whom he had trained in politics were busy in seeking their own advancement, which was not to be promoted by tears for a fallen minister; the people had never loved him, and were indifferent about one who was no longer powerful. In a time of universal uncertainty every one was speculating on the future, and saw that the future was not to be determined by Wolsey or by Wolsey's ideas. Not without reason has the story of Wolsey's fall passed into a parable of the heartlessness of the world.

For Wolsey lived for the world as few men have ever done; not for the larger world of intellectual thought or spiritual aspiration, but for the actual, immediate world of affairs. He limited himself to its problems, but within its limits he took a wider and juster view of the problems of his time than any English statesman has ever done. For politics in the largest sense, comprising all the relations of the nation at home and abroad, Wolsey had a capacity which amounted to genius, and it is doubtful if this can be said of any other Englishman. There have been many capable administrators, many excellent organisers, many who bravely faced the difficulties of their time, many who advocated particular reforms and achieved definite results. But Wolsey aimed at doing all these things together and more. Taking England as he found her, he aimed at developing all her latent possibilities, and leading Europe to follow in her train. In this project there was nothing chimerical or fantastic, for Wolsey's mind was eminently practical. Starting from the existing condition of affairs, he made England for a time the centre of European politics, and gave her an influence far higher than she could claim on material grounds. Moreover, his far-reaching schemes abroad did not interfere with strict attention to the details of England's interests. His foreign policy was to promote English trade, facilitate the union of Scotland, keep peace at small expense, prepare the way for internal re-organisation, and secure the right of dealing judiciously with ecclesiastical reform. Wolsey's plans all hung together. However absorbed he might be in a particular point it was only part of a great design, and he used each advantage which he gained as a means of strengthening England's position for some future undertaking. He had a clear view of the future as a whole; he knew not only what he wished to make of England but of Europe as well. He never worked at a question from one motive only; what failed for one purpose was made useful for another; his resources were not bounded by the immediate result.

Politics to him was not a pursuit, it was a passion. He loved it as an artist loves his art, for he found in it a complete satisfaction for his nature. All that was best, and all that was worst, in Wolsey sprang from this exceptional attitude towards statecraft, which he practised with enthusiasm, not in the spirit of cold calculation. The world is accustomed to statesmen who clothe the results of calculation in the language of enthusiasm; Wolsey's language was practical and direct, his passionate aspirations were restrained within his own bosom.

Thus there is a largeness and distinction about Wolsey's aims, a far-reaching patriotism, and an admirable lucidity. He was indeed a political artist, who worked with a free hand and a certain touch. He was absorbed in his art as a painter over his picture, and he did not shrink as the full size of his canvas was gradually enrolled. He set himself to dominate Europe, and was fearless and self-contained. He gave himself entirely to his work, and in his eyes the nobility of his end justified any means. But he was sensitive, as all artists are, and could not work under cramped conditions. When he was restricted to the small matter of the divorce his hand lost its cunning. He was, though he knew it not, fitted to serve England, but not fitted to serve the English king. He had the aims of a national statesman, not of a royal servant.

Wolsey's misfortune was that his lot was cast on days when the career of a statesman was not distinct from that of a royal servant. He owed his introduction to politics solely to royal favour, and neither had nor could obtain any other warrant for his position. For good or evil England was identified with her king, and it was long before it could be otherwise. Certainly Wolsey had no wish that it should be otherwise, and his subservience to the royal will seems to us to be unworthy of his greatness. But Wolsey associated his political life with the king's goodwill, and Henry was to him a symbol of all that was best and most intelligent in England. His deviations from his own policy in obedience to the king were not more degrading or more inevitable than are the calculations of the modern statesman about the exact limits of the field of practical politics. A statesman has not only to form projects, he has to secure a force behind him which will enable him to give them effect. Each age recognises this fact, and acts accordingly. There is nothing more intrinsically base in Wolsey's subservience to the royal will than in the efforts of modern statesmen to bid against one another for an opportunity of carrying out what they think to be the will of the people. No politician has a complete command of his field of action ; his highmindedness and purity must be tested by the degree of compromise which consciously or unconsciously he makes between his love of power and his knowledge or his conscience. The utmost that can be demanded of him is that he should not, to keep his place, deliberately act contrary to what he believes to be wise or knows to be right.

In his general conduct of politics Wolsey was true to his principles, and though occasionally thwarted, he still pursued the same ends. The matter of the divorce was sprung upon him, and it would have been well for Wolsey's fame if he had retired rather than involve himself in the unworthy proceedings to which it led. But

the temptation to all men to think themselves necessary
in the sphere which they have made their own is a subtle
one; and those who begin by hoping that they may
minimise inevitable mischief, end by being dragged into
the mire. To a statesman this temptation is great in
proportion to the largeness of his ultimate aim. He
resents that his schemes should be ruined by a temporary
derangement of the perspective of affairs; he believes
that his practised hand can easily solve a trumpery
difficulty; the excellence of his intentions in the long-
run justifies an occasional sacrifice on the shrine of
present necessity. If he does some things amiss, after
all he is not responsible for them; they are disagreeable
incidents in his tenure of office.

So Wolsey regarded the divorce; and he is not greatly
to be blamed for agreeing to promote it. He saw great
national advantages in a divorce; he knew that it
would be well for England if Henry VIII. left male
issue; he did not like the political influence of Katharine;
he saw that Henry was not likely to be happy in her
society. It would have been difficult for him to find in
the proposal itself a sufficient reason for withdrawing
from politics even if he could have done so with safety.
Not even Wolsey could foresee the king's obstinacy and
tenacity of purpose, the depth of meanness to which he
would sink, and to which he would drag all around him.
Wolsey found himself powerless to resist, and 'the
growing consciousness of moral turpitude practised to no
purpose degraded him in his own eyes and robbed him
of his strength. When once the divorce question was
started Wolsey was pushed on to his ruin by a power
of imperious wickedness which debased others without

losing its own self-respect. The dictates of public opinion are, after all, not so very different from the commands of an absolute king. Both may destroy their victims, and go on their own way with heads erect.

So when we speak of the fall of Wolsey we mean more than his irrevocable loss of power. He had lost his inner strength, and no longer kept his hold upon affairs. He knew that he was sullied and unnerved; that he had sunk from the position of a leader to that of one who tremblingly follows and devises shifty plans that he may still exercise the semblance of his old authority. He knew that in his negotiations about the divorce he staked everything that · he had gained, and that the result, whatever it was, would be disastrous to his great designs. If he had succeeded he would have degraded the Papacy; and when Henry had once learned how easy it was for him to get his own way, he would have used his knowledge to the full, and Wolsey would have been powerless to direct him. When Wolsey became the instrument of the king's self-will, he hoped that a few disappointments would wear out his obstinacy; when he saw Henry's growing resoluteness and complete self-will he knew that for himself the future was hopeless. Still he had not the magnanimity to resign himself to his disappointment He clung to power when power had ceased to be useful for his plans. He clung to power, because the habits of office had become to him a second nature. He vainly strove to find satisfaction in the discharge of his episcopal duties; he vainly tried to content himself with the simple affairs of simple men. He had given himself entirely to the material world, and had estranged himself from the spiritual world, which

was to him thin and unsubstantial to the last. He
could not refrain from casting longing glances behind
him, and his last days are pitiable. The words of the
dying man are often quoted as showing the misery of
those who trust in princes' favour. But they are not
merely an echo of a far-off state of things which has
passed by for ever. "To serve one's country" may have a
loftier and more noble sound than "to serve one's king,"
but the meaning is not necessarily different. The
thought in Wolsey's heart was this—"If I had served
the spiritual interests of my country as I have striven to
serve its material interests my conscience would be
more at rest." For Wolsey was a true patriot, and had
noble aims. Much as he might deaden his conscience,
he did not extinguish it; and his last judgment of
himself expressed the sad conviction that neither his
patriotism nor the nobility of his aims had saved him
from actions which he could not justify, and which his
conscience loudly condemned.

We have called Wolsey a political artist: and this,
which makes his career attractive, is the secret of his
unpopularity. Wolsey's designs did not arise from
the pressure of absolute necessity, and their meaning
was not apparent to his contemporaries. Englishmen
thought then, as they think now, that England should
disregard foreign affairs and develop her own resources;
or if foreign affairs are undertaken they demand the
success of English arms, and claim to be repaid in current
coin or palpable advantages. Wolsey believed that the
establishment of England's power on the Continent was
necessary for the increase of English trade, and was a
preliminary for the wise solution of those questions which

were most urgent in domestic politics. He was the last English statesman of the old school, which regarded England not as a separate nation, but as an integral part of Western Christendom. He did not look upon questions as being solely English questions : he did not aim merely at reforming English monasteries or asserting a new position for the English Church. But he thought that England was ripe for practically carrying out reforms which had long been talked of, and remedying abuses which had long been lamented ; and he hoped that England in these respects would serve as a model to the rest of Europe. Only if England was in full accord with European sentiment, was powerful, and was respected, could this be done. Wolsey did not prefer foreign politics on their own account, but he found them to be the necessary preliminary for any lasting work on the lines which he contemplated. As regards Church matters he was strictly practical. He had no belief in reforming councils, or pragmatic sanctions, or Gallican liberties; he cared little for England's weapon of *præmunire*. He did not look upon the Pope as a powerful adversary who was to be held at arm's length ; he regarded him as a man to be managed and converted into a useful ally. Wolsey was entirely Erastian. Power was to him the important thing in human affairs, and all power was the same; he believed much more in the divine right of Henry VIII. than in the divine right of Clement VII. merely because Henry's power seemed to him practically to be greater. However poetical Wolsey's main ideas might be, he had no illusions about the actual facts of politics.

The Englishmen of his own day did not appreciate

Wolsey's aims, and supposed that his foreign policy was for the gratification of his own vanity, or was the result of a desire to gain the Papacy. No one understood him in his own time. He bore the burden of everything that was done, and all the causes of popular discontent were laid at his door. If the loyalty of Wolsey seems strange to our eyes, still more inexplicable is the loyalty of the English people, who could believe in Henry's good intentions, and could suppose that he was entirely ruled by Wolsey contrary to his own inclinations. Wolsey was universally hated; by the nobles as an upstart, by the people as a tyrant, by Churchmen as a dangerous reformer, by the Lutherans as a rank Papist. While he was in power he kept in restraint various elements of disorder; but he shared the fate of those who rule without identifying themselves with any party. When his power came to an end no minister could assume his place or pick up the threads which fell from his hands. It was left to Henry VIII., who had learned more from Wolsey than any one else, to direct England's fortunes on a lower level of endeavour. We may admire his clear head and his strong hand; we may even prefer the results of his solution to those which Wolsey would have wrought; but we must confess that personal motives held the chief place in his mind, and that considerations of the common weal came only in the second place. For Henry VIII. abandoned Wolsey's idea of a European settlement of ecclesiastical questions, and gradually undertook a national settlement on lines drawn solely with reference to his own desires and his own interest. In this simpler matter it was possible for him to enjoy some measure of success, and this was chiefly due to the

preparation which Wolsey had made. For the work of
a statesman is never entirely thrown away; if his own
plans fail, he leaves the way open for others who may
use his means for widely different ends.

Wolsey was the creator of the forces which worked
the great change in England in the sixteenth century.
He obtained for England a position in the esteem of
Europe which he had meant to use for the direction
of Europe generally. Henry used that position for
the assertion of England's right to settle its own affairs
for itself; and the position proved strong enough to
ward off foreign interference, and to carry England safely
through the first period of a dangerous crisis. It was
because Wolsey had laid a sure foundation that England
emerged from her separatist policy, isolated, it is true,
but not excluded from European influence. Again,
Wolsey exalted the royal power, because he believed
that it alone could rise above the separate interests of
classes, and could give a large expression to the national
weal. Henry profited by Wolsey's labours to pursue
exclusively his own interests, yet he learned enough
to interweave them dexterously with some national interests in such a way that they could not practically be
disentangled, and that he had sufficient adherents to put
down opposition when it arose. Even the preliminary
steps which Wolsey had taken were carefully followed.
His scheme for the gradual conversion of monasteries
into more useful institutions was revived, and men believed that it would be imitated: the very agents that
he had trained for the work of turning monasteries into
educational establishments were employed in sweeping
the monastic revenues into the royal coffers. So it

was with all other things. Henry learned Wolsey's methods, and popularised Wolsey's phrases. He clothed his own self-seeking with the dignity of Wolsey's designs; the hands were the hands of Henry, but the voice was an echo of the voice of Wolsey.

The new England that was created in the sixteenth century was strangely unlike that which Wolsey had dreamed of, yet none the less it was animated by his spirit. His ideal of England, influential in Europe through the mediatorial policy which her insular position allowed her to claim, prosperous at home through the influence which she obtained by her far-sighted wisdom and disinterestedness—this is Wolsey's permanent contribution to the history of English politics.

INDEX

ADRIAN VI., Pope, election of, 87, 88; enters league against France, 96; death of, 99.

Agostino, Wolsey's physician, 199, 200

Albany, James, Duke of, made Regent of Scotland, 69; allied with Queen Margaret, 91; retreats before Lord Dacre, 92; retires from Wark, 98; recalled to France, 107.

Alcock, John, Bishop of Ely, 141.

Amicable Loan, 111, 112.

Angus, Archibald, Earl of, marries Queen-Dowager Margaret, 69, in France and England, 107.

Ardres, fortification of, 68.

BAINBRIDGE, Thomas, Archbishop of York, 29-39.

Blunt, Elizabeth, 118.

Boleyn, Anne, Henry VIII.'s passion for, 152; her influence over Henry VIII., 159, 160, 165-168.

Bourbon, Constable of, revolts from Francis I., 94; negotiations of Pace with, 106, 107; in Italy, 121

Bruges, Wolsey meets Charles V at, 77, 78.

Buckingham, Duke of, executed, 70, 71

Buttes, Doctor, 192, 193.

CALAIS, meeting of Henry VIII. and Charles V. at, 63; conference at, 73-82.

Cambrai, League of, 8, 9, 14, 15; conference at, 177, 178

Campeggio, Cardinal, sent to England, 164, 165; his action about the divorce, 171-173; his interview with Henry VIII., 181, seizure of his baggage, 182, 183.

Cardinal College, 143, 144, 196

Carey, Eleanor, 166.

Cavendish, George, memoir of Wolsey quoted, 156, 158, 175, 200-205; his interview with Henry VIII., 207, 208; later life of, 209.

Cawood Castle, Wolsey at, 197, 199-201.

Charles, Prince of Castile, betrothed to Mary of England, 32; betrothed to Renée of France, 37, King of Spain, 44; goes to Spain, 46, elected Emperor Charles V., 52-54, seeks interview with Henry VIII., 58; pensions Wolsey, 59; in England, 61; meets Henry VIII at Calais, 63; his marriage projects, 67; attacked by Francis I, 72; meets Wolsey at Bruges, 77, 78, his policy in papal election, 85-88; visits London, 89; allied with Henry VIII.,

90; negotiations with, about marriage, 116-118; makes peace of Cambrai, 178.

Charles VIII., 6.

Chièvres, death of, 74.

Clement VII., Pope, attacked in Rome, 121; visited by Knight at Orvieto, 160; embassy of Gardiner to, 163, 164; his hesitation about the divorce, 172.

Cromwell, Thomas, early life of, 188; parts from Wolsey, 189; speaks in Wolsey's behalf, 191.

DACRE, Lord, Warden of the Western Marches, 70; defends Carlisle against Albany, 92.

De Praet, 108, 109.

Dorset, Marquis of, 19; commands in Guienne, 23.

ERASMUS, 140.

Esher, Wolsey at, 189, 192, 193.

FERDINAND, King of Aragon, 5; allied with Maximilian, 14; joins Holy League, 16; deserts Henry VIII. in Guienne, 23, allies with France, 27; dies, 44.

Fisher, John, Bishop of Rochester, 145, 155, 156, 175.

Fitzroy, Henry, Duke of Richmond, 118.

Flodden Field, Battle of, 26.

Fox, Richard, Bishop of Winchester, 20, 22, 137, 141.

Francis I., King of France, accession of, 35, 36; wins Duchy of Milan, 38; makes treaty of Noyon, 44; candidate for the empire, 52-55; seeks interview with Henry VIII., 57; pensions Wolsey, 59; at Field of Cloth of Gold, 62; attacks Charles V., 72; his unpopularity, 90; captured at Pavia, 109; signs treaty of Madrid, 120; makes peace with England, 122; interview of Wolsey with, at Amiens, 157; makes peace of Cambrai, 178.

Fiundsberg, George, 121.

GARDINER, Stephen, ambassador to Clement VII., 161-163; king's favourite, 176; made Bishop of Winchester, 190.

Gattinara, Ercurino della, negotiates with Tunstal, 68; his position with Charles V, 75; at conference of Calais, 76, 77, 79, 80.

Gigli, Silvestro dei, Bishop of Worcester, 29, 38.

Greene, John, 113.

Guienne, scheme for conquest of, 16, 17; its failure, 23.

Guisnes, 61, 62

HAMPTON COURT, 116.

Henry VII., policy of, 10, 11, 20, 21-30, 124

Henry VIII., accession of, 11; joins Holy League, 16; his Council, 22; his expedition into France, 25; abandoned by Ferdinand and Maximilian, 28; allies with Louis XII., 32-35; asks for Wolsey's cardinalate, 33, 39; his dealings with Maximilian, 41-45; a candidate for the empire, 53-55; allies with Charles V., 90; costliness of his policy, 102; his management of Parliament, 129; question of his divorce, 151; rebukes Wolsey, 167-170; his last interview with Wolsey, 181, 182

Howard, Sir Edward, 24.

IPSWICH, 18; college of, 143, 195.

Isabella of Portugal, 117.

JAMES V. set up King of Scotland, 108.

Jordan, Isabella, 166.

Julius II., Pope, and Italian politics, 9, 15

KATHARINE, Queen of England, 13, 16 ; confides in Wolsey, 25 , Regent of England, 26 ; opposed to French alliance, 60 ; signs of her breach with king, 118 ; divorce question moved, 151-153 ; her attitude before the legatine court, 174.
Kingston, Sir William, 202-207.
Knight, secretary, sent to Rome, 158-161.

LADY MARGARET PROFESSORSHIPS, 145.
League, the Italian, 6, 7
—— of Cambrai, 8, 9, 14, 15.
—— the Holy, 16.
Legate, Wolsey nominated, 50 ; his legatine courts, 147.
Leicester Abbey, death of Wolsey at, 203-206.
Leo X., Pope, accession of, 27 ; refuses Wolsey's cardinalate, 33, 34 ; creates Wolsey cardinal, 39 ; annoyed at Wolsey's success, 50 ; sides with Charles V., 66, 73, 74 ; death of, 85.
Lincoln, Wolsey Dean of, 22 ; Bishop of, 29.
Longueville, Duke of, 32
Louis XI., King of France, his policy, 5.
Louis XII., King of France, and League of Cambrai, 9, 10 ; his dealings with Julius II., 15 ; defeated in Italy, 25 , makes truce with Ferdinand and Maximilian, 28 ; marries Mary of England, 33 ; dies, 34.
Louise of Savoy, mother of Francis I., makes peace with England, 119.
Lymington, Wolsey Vicar of, 19.

MADRID, Treaty of, 120.
Magdalen College, Oxford, 18, 19.
Margaret, queen of James IV. of Scotland, marries Earl of Angus,

69 ; allies with Albany, 91 ; managed by Wolsey, 108.
Marignano, battle of, 38.
Mary, Princess, daughter of Henry VII., married to Louis XII., 32 ; marries Duke of Suffolk, 37.
Mary, Princess, daughter of Henry VIII., married by proxy to Dauphin, 49 ; betrothed to Charles V., 63, 64 ; betrothed to Duke of Orleans, 122.
Maximilian, Emperor, joins Italian League, 6 , allied with Ferdinand, 14 ; relations of Henry VII. with, 21 ; at Terouenne, 25 ; deserts Henry VIII., 27, 28 ; makes a futile expedition against Milan, 40 - 42 ; signs peace of Noyon, 45 ; dies, 52.
Medici, Guilio dei, candidate for the Papacy, 87 ; elected Clement VII., 99, 100.
Montdidier, capture of, 97.
More, Sir Thomas, Speaker in 1523, 103-105 ; Chancellor, 190.

NANFAN, Sir Richard, 19.
Norfolk, Thomas Howard I., Duke of, 30, 34.
Norfolk, Thomas Howard II., Duke of, puts down tumult, 113, 114; plots against Wolsey, 177, 181 , receives great seal from Wolsey, 186 ; president of the Council, 190.
Norwich, tumult in, 113.
Noyon, Treaty of, 44, 45.

OXFORD, Wolsey's influence in, 145-147.

PACE, Richard, his mission to Maximilian, 41-43 ; mission to the German Elector, 55 ; mission to Venice, 95 ; mission to Bourbon, 106, 107.
Parliament, of 1523, 103, 105 , Wolsey's attitude to, 129, 130

Paulet, Sir Amyas, 19.
Pavia, battle of, 109.
Picardy, invasion of, 90.
Putney, Wolsey at, 187

RHODES captured by Turks, 93
Richmond Lodge, Wolsey at, 193.
Ruthal, Bishop of Durham, 22.

ST. ALBAN'S, Wolsey made Abbot of, 83.
Sanctuary, right of, 135.
Scrooby, Wolsey at, 195.
Sheffield Park, Wolsey at, 202
Southwell, Wolsey at, 194.
Spinelly, Thomas, 31.
Standish, Henry, 135-138
Stile, John, 31.
Suffolk, Charles Brandon, Duke of, 30 ; ambassador to France, 36 ; marries Mary of England, 37 ; commander in France, 97 ; insults Wolsey, 176 ; receives great seal from Wolsey, 186.
Surrey, Thomas Howard I., Earl of, member of Henry VII.'s Council, 22, 23 ; created Duke of Norfolk (q v) 1514.
Surrey, Thomas Howard II , Earl of, commander in France, 90, 91 ; put in charge of the Border,

92; takes the field against Albany, 98 ; succeeded Duke of Norfolk (q.v.) 1524.
Swiss troops in Milan, 38, 41, 42.

TEROUENNE, capture of, 25.
Tournai, capture of, 25 ; Wolsey, Bishop of, 29 , ceded to France, 47-49 ; captured by, 81
Tunstal, Cuthbert, ambassador to Charles V., 67, 68; speech as chancellor, 103.

VENICE, attacked by League of Cambrai, 8, 9 ; England's dealings with, 95, 96.
Vives, Juan Luis, 146.

WALSHE, Sir Walter, 199.
Walsingham, Wolsey's pilgrimage to, 47.
Warham, Archbishop, 20, 147, 154, 155.
Wingfield, Sir Richard, 31, 41-43, 116.
Worms, Diet of, 73.
Wykeham, William of, 141.

YORK, archbishopric of, given to Wolsey, 29.

THE END

Printed by R. & R. CLARK, LIMITED, *Edinburgh.*

BY THE SAME AUTHOR.

HISTORY OF ROME

With Maps.

Pott 8vo.   Sewed, 1s. 6d. ; *Stiff Boards,* 1s. 9d.

[*Literature Primers.*

SATURDAY REVIEW.—" Mr. Creighton is constantly stopping to gather up the threads into his reader's hands, to mark ' noticeable points,' to give systematic little bits of generalisation about causes, and little lists of questions that a boy should bear in mind throughout ; and all this is consistently couched in the *lenior imperativus* of the lecturer. . . . The book is, as a rule, uniformly good, and far ahead of any small school histories that have appeared before."

ACADEMY.—" Mr. Creighton's ' History of Rome ' reminds us once more that, in the matter of historical handbooks at least, we boast to be much better than our fathers. At the outset he touches the right chord by pointing out that the explanation of many important facts in modern Europe is to be sought in the history of old Rome, and he proceeds by a judicious selection of facts to bring into relief those social and political changes which are the true subjects of history. But Mr. Creighton takes care not to fall into the mistake of omitting the tales which have been enjoyed by so many generations, and in spite of his cramped space he finds room for Cincinnatus at the Plough and the Schoolmaster of Falerii."

SCHOOL BOARD CHRONICLE.—" The author has been curiously successful in telling in this intelligent way the story of Rome from first to last in a rudimentary shilling book of little more than a hundred and twenty pages, with maps, tables, and a brief chronology."

MACMILLAN AND CO., Ltd., LONDON.

Twelve English Statesmen

Edited by Viscount MORLEY.

Crown 8vo. 3s. *net each*

WILLIAM THE CONQUEROR. By Edward A. Freeman, D.C.L., LL.D.

TIMES.—"Gives with great picturesqueness . . . the dramatic incidents of a memorable career far removed from our times and our manner of thinking."

HENRY II. By Mrs. J. R. Green.

TIMES.—"It is delightfully real and readable, and in spite of severe compression has the charm of a mediæval romance."

EDWARD I. By Professor T. F. Tout, M.A.

SPEAKER.—"A truer or more life-like picture of the king, the conqueror, the overlord, the duke, has never yet been drawn."

HENRY VII. By Dr James Gairdner.

ATHENÆUM.—"The best account of Henry VII. that has yet appeared.

CARDINAL WOLSEY. By Bishop Creighton, D.D.

SATURDAY REVIEW.—"Is exactly what one of a series of short biographies of English Statesmen ought to be."

ELIZABETH. By E. S. Beesly, M.A.

MANCHESTER GUARDIAN.—"It may be recommended as the best and briefest and most trustworthy of the many books that in this generation have dealt with the life and deeds of that 'bright Occidental Star, Queen Elizabeth of happy memory.'"

OLIVER CROMWELL. By Frederic Harrison.

TIMES.—"Gives a wonderfully vivid picture of events."

WILLIAM III. By H. D. Traill.

SPECTATOR.—"Mr. Traill has done his work well in the limited space at his command. The narrative portion is clear and vivacious, and his criticisms, although sometimes trenchant, are substantially just."

WALPOLE. By Viscount Morley.

ST. JAMES'S GAZETTE—"It deserves to be read, not only as the work of one of the most prominent politicians of the day, but for its intrinsic merits. It is a clever, thoughtful, and interesting biography."

PITT. By Lord Rosebery.

TIMES.—"Brilliant and fascinating. . . . The style is terse, masculine, nervous, articulate, and clear; the grasp of circumstance and character is firm, penetrating, luminous, and unprejudiced; the judgment is broad, generous, humane, and scrupulously candid. . . . It is not only a luminous estimate of Pitt's character and policy; it is also a brilliant gallery of portraits. The portrait of Fox, for example, is a masterpiece."

PEEL. By Sir J. R. Thursfield, M.A.

DAILY NEWS.—"A model of what such a book should be. We can give it no higher praise than to say that it is worthy to rank with Mr. John Morley's *Walpole* in the same series."

CHATHAM. By Frederic Harrison.

ST. JAMES'S GAZETTE.—"It comes near the model of what such a book should be"

MACMILLAN AND CO., Ltd., LONDON

𝔉oreign 𝔖tatesmen 𝔖eries.

Edited by J. B. BURY, LL.D., Regius Professor of Modern History at Cambridge.

Crown 8vo. 3s. net each.

CHARLES THE GREAT. By THOMAS HODGKIN, D.C.L., Author of *Italy and her Invaders*, etc.

PHILIP AUGUSTUS. By The Very Rev. W. H. HUTTON.

WILLIAM THE SILENT. By FREDERIC HARRISON.

PHILIP THE SECOND OF SPAIN. By Major MARTIN HUME.

RICHELIEU. By R. LODGE, Professor of History in the University of Edinburgh.

MARIA THERESA. By J. FRANCK BRIGHT, D.D

JOSEPH II. By J. FRANCK BRIGHT, D D.

MIRABEAU. By P F. WILLERT, Fellow of Exeter College, Oxford.

COSIMO DE MEDICI. By Miss K. D EWART.

CAVOUR. By the Countess MARTINENGO CESARESCO.

MAZARIN. By ARTHUR HASSALL, Student and Tutor of Christ Church, Oxford.

MACMILLAN AND CO., LTD., LONDON.

English Men of Letters.

NEW SERIES

Crown 8vo. Gilt tops. Flat backs. 3s. net each.

MATTHEW ARNOLD. By HERBERT W PAUL.

JANE AUSTEN. By F. WARRE CORNISH.

SIR THOMAS BROWNE. By EDMUND GOSSE.

BROWNING. By G. K. CHESTERTON.

FANNY BURNEY. By AUSTIN DOBSON.

CRABBE. By ALFRED AINGER.

MARIA EDGEWORTH. By the Hon. EMILY LAWLESS.

GEORGE ELIOT. By Sir LESLIE STEPHEN, K.C.B.

EDWARD FITZGERALD. By A. C. BENSON.

HAZLITT. By AUGUSTINE BIRRELL, K.C.

HOBBES. By Sir LESLIE STEPHEN, K.C.B.

BEN JONSON. By G. GREGORY SMITH.

ANDREW MARVELL. By AUGUSTINE BIRRELL, K.C.

THOMAS MOORE. By STEPHEN GWYNN.

WILLIAM MORRIS. By ALFRED NOYES.

WALTER PATER. By A. C. BENSON.

RICHARDSON. By AUSTIN DOBSON.

ROSSETTI. By A. C. BENSON.

RUSKIN. By FREDERIC HARRISON.

SHAKESPEARE. By Sir WALTER RALEIGH.

ADAM SMITH. By FRANCIS W. HIRST.

SYDNEY SMITH. By GEORGE W. E RUSSELL.

JEREMY TAYLOR. By EDMUND GOSSE.

TENNYSON. By Sir ALFRED LYALL.

JAMES THOMSON. By G. C. MACAULAY.

MACMILLAN AND CO., LTD., LONDON.

English Men of Letters.

EDITED BY VISCOUNT MORLEY

Library Edition. Crown 8vo. 3s. net.

Pocket Edition. Fcap. 8vo. Special Cover Design. Cloth, 2s. net.

ADDISON.
By W. J. COURTHOPE.

BACON.
By Dean CHURCH.

BENTLEY.
By Sir RICHARD JEBB.

BUNYAN.
By J. A. FROUDE.

BURKE.
By Viscount MORLEY.

BURNS.
By Prof. J. C. SHAIRP.

BYRON.
By Professor J. NICHOL.

CARLYLE.
By Professor J. NICHOL.

CHAUCER.
By Sir A. W. WARD.

COLERIDGE.
By H. D. TRAILL.

COWPER.
By GOLDWIN SMITH.

DEFOE.
By W. MINTO.

DE QUINCEY.
By Professor D. MASSON.

DICKENS.
By Sir A. W. WARD.

DRYDEN.
By G. SAINTSBURY.

FIELDING.
By AUSTIN DOBSON.

GIBBON.
By J. COTTER MORISON.

GOLDSMITH.
By W. BLACK.

GRAY.
By EDMUND GOSSE.

HAWTHORNE.
By HENRY JAMES.

HUME.
By Professor HUXLEY, F.R.S.

JOHNSON.
By Sir LESLIE STEPHEN, K.C.B.

KEATS.
By Sir SIDNEY COLVIN.

LAMB, CHARLES.
By Canon AINGER.

LANDOR.
By Sir SIDNEY COLVIN.

LOCKE.
By THOMAS FOWLER.

MACAULAY.
By J. COTTER MORISON.

MILTON.
By MARK PATTISON.

POPE.
By Sir LESLIE STEPHEN, K.C.B.

SCOTT.
By R. H. HUTTON.

SHELLEY.
By J. A. SYMONDS.

SHERIDAN.
By Mrs. OLIPHANT.

SIDNEY.
By J. A. SYMONDS.

SOUTHEY.
By Professor E. DOWDEN.

SPENSER.
By Dean CHURCH.

STERNE.
By H. D. TRAILL.

SWIFT.
By Sir LESLIE STEPHEN, K.C.B.

THACKERAY.
By ANTHONY TROLLOPE.

WORDSWORTH.
By F. W. H. MYERS.

MACMILLAN AND CO., LTD., LONDON.

English Men of Action Series.

Crown 8vo. Cloth. With Portraits. 3s. net each.

COLIN CAMPBELL. By ARCHIBALD FORBES.

CLIVE. By Sir CHARLES WILSON.

CAPTAIN COOK. By Sir WALTER BESANT.

DAMPIER. By W. CLARK RUSSELL

DRAKE. By Sir JULIAN CORBETT.

DUNDONALD. By the Hon. J. W. FORTESCUE.

GENERAL GORDON. By Sir W. BUTLER.

WARREN HASTINGS. By Sir A. LYALL

SIR HENRY HAVELOCK. By ARCHIBALD FORBES.

HENRY V. By the Rev. A. J. CHURCH.

LORD LAWRENCE. By Sir RICHARD TEMPLE.

LIVINGSTONE. By THOMAS HUGHES.

MONK. By Sir JULIAN CORBETT.

MONTROSE. By MOWBRAY MORRIS.

SIR CHARLES NAPIER. By Sir W. BUTLER.

NELSON. By Sir J. K. LAUGHTON.

PETERBOROUGH. By W. STEBBING.

SIR WALTER RALEIGH. By Sir RENNELL RODD

RODNEY. By DAVID HANNAY.

CAPTAIN JOHN SMITH. By A. G. BRADLEY

STRAFFORD. By H. D. TRAILL.

WARWICK, the King-Maker. By Sir C. W. OMAN.

WELLINGTON. By GEORGE HOOPER.

WOLFE. By A. G. BRADLEY.

MACMILLAN AND CO., LTD., LONDON.

CPSIA information can be obtained
at www.ICGtesting.com
Printed in the USA
LVOW13*1339280518

578722LV00022B/795/P

9 781347 257906